Brilliant Thinker

How to be a
Brilliant
Thinker

Exercise your mind and find creative solutions

Paul Sloane

KoganPage

London and Philadelphia

For Ann, Jackie, Val, Hannah and everyone who strives to be brilliant

First published in Great Britain and the United States in 2010 by Kogan Page Limited

120 Pentonville Road
London N1 9JN
United Kingdom
www.koganpage.com

525 South 4th Street, #241
Philadelphia PA 19147
USA

© Paul Sloane, 2010

ISBN 978 0 7494 5506 4
E-ISBN 978 0 7494 5888 1

British Library Cataloguing-in-Publication Data

A CIP record for this book is available from the British Library.

Library of Congress Cataloging-in-Publication Data
Sloane, Paul, 1950-
      How to be a brilliant thinker : exercise your mind and find creative solutions / Paul Sloane.
         p. cm.
      Includes bibliographical references and index.
      ISBN 978-0-7494-5506-4
   1. Thought and thinking. 2. Creative thinking. 3. Lateral thinking. I. Title.
      BF441.S597 2010
      153.4'2—dc22
                                                2009028714

Typeset by JS Typesetting Ltd, Porthcawl, Mid Glamorgan
Printed and bound in India by Replika Press Pvt Ltd

Contents

Foreword

One of the most fortunate moments of my life, a moment of pure serendipity, was when I found myself seated next to Paul Sloane at a conference dinner. One position more to the left or to the right and we might never have met. We started talking and it turned out that we were both interested in thinking, especially lateral thinking. So began a collaboration that has lasted many years and has resulted in over a dozen books of lateral thinking puzzles. I have learnt a great deal about thinking from Paul and maybe he has learnt a little from me too. In our case, two heads have been vastly better than one.

Clever thinking is one of the main reasons why we of the human race have survived so long as a species against all the odds. Using our brains, we have come to understand Nature, the elements, our environment, disease, energy, the food chain, and many other entities that can both threaten and enhance our continued existence. There is of course a great deal more left to understand and explore, but we are now in a better position than ever before to deepen our understanding and extend the boundaries of exploration because we are able to think about thinking.

In this book, *How to Be a Brilliant Thinker*, Paul Sloane has produced a very comprehensive guidebook to the art of thinking, which avoids the faults of the many such books others have written. On the one hand it is sound on theory, and on the other hand, and perhaps more importantly, it is laced with practical suggestions and real-life examples of how great thinkers, even from the ranks of ordinary people, opened up their minds to new and exciting thought processes and prospered in various ways. I believe it would be impossible for anyone to read this book and absorb its contents and not become a better and more brilliant thinker.

I teach a course on problem solving at University College Cork and, although the module is part of a mathematics degree, the class inevitably discusses problems in general and how to solve them. The world is beset with many major problems crying out for solution – global warming, poverty, the food supply, the scourge of drugs, preservation of peace, and many others (as an exercise, list what you think are the major problems facing the world). We desperately need new and creative solutions to these problems and new modes of thinking –– analytical, lateral, humorous, and all the other approaches described in this book. Young minds with their fresh approach have of course a vital role to play, but so does the older generation. Much of our present thinking is in fact redundant. Just as people who lose their jobs need to retrain and acquire new skills, we need to retrain our thinking.

And let me let you into a little secret – you can be as brilliant a thinker as anyone else if you put the work into practice and extend your existing skills as part of a lifelong learning strategy. What's more, it can be a lot of fun developing your thinking skills, just about the most fun you can have with your clothes on. Enjoy the exercise!

Des MacHale
Author and Associate Professor of Mathematics at
University College Cork

1

The need for different thinking

We are creatures of habit. Each day we wake up on the same side of the bed. We put on the same type of clothes we wore the previous day, we eat the same type of breakfast, we sit in the same car and we take the same route to work or school. When we get there we think in the same way as we thought the previous day. Most of our thinking is in the same groove – it is analytical, convergent, critical, left-brain thinking. This is our normal mode of operation and it is hard to appreciate just how severely we hamper ourselves by restricting our thinking in this way. There are many other ways of thinking and of expressing our thoughts.

We express our thinking in words. It seems so natural to say things, to use words and to write routine memos, e-mails and reports that we rarely stop to ask if there is a better way to do things. But mathematicians express themselves with equations, accountants with numbers, artists with pictures, composers with music, architects with drawings, engineers with models, movie directors with moving images, and public speakers with oratory and stories. Why do we so rarely borrow any of their forms of expression?

In this book we will explore different kinds of thinking and other approaches to some of the mental challenges we face. Let's start with convergent and divergent thinking. Convergent thinking is our normal state. When we hear a suggestion, our instincts are to examine it, criticize it and analyse its consequences with particular emphasis on what might be wrong with it. We are trained at school and university to summarize, scrutinize and evaluate the works of authors, historians and scientists. It is easy and natural for us to focus in on a notion and examine it critically from various viewpoints. We bring our own assumptions and mindset to bear and put the new idea into the framework of the world as we see it.

Divergent thinking, on the other hand, involves moving away from the core subject in a spread of directions. When we use divergent thinking we can generate all sorts of ideas that are not obviously connected with the original challenge or concept. We stretch the boundaries and let our imagination generate many different possibilities – including wild or unsound ideas. It is the counterpoint to convergent thinking, where we focus sharply on one target and narrow down our options to arrive at a chosen solution.

Furthermore we have a very disturbing tendency to see and gather only evidence that supports our existing beliefs and to reject or ignore evidence that conflicts with our beliefs. This was demonstrated in a famous psychology experiment by Peter Wason at the University of London. He showed undergraduate students a sequence of three numbers – 2, 4, 6 – and said that they conformed to a rule that he had chosen. The student's task was to deduce what the rule was by trying sets of three numbers. For each try, Wason would tell them whether it conformed to the rule or not. They could try a few times and then attempt to guess the rule. In almost every case the student would try a similar set of numbers – say 6, 8, 10. Watson would advise that this met the rule and the student would guess that the rule was that the numbers had to increase by 2. This was incorrect. The student would then try another set of numbers – say 3, 6, 9. Again Wason would say that this conformed to the rule. The student would then say the rule is 1x, 2x, 3x. This was again incorrect and so it would go on. The students were fixated by finding a regular pattern of incremental numbers and always tried a set of numbers that met their anticipated rule. In fact the rule that Wason used was that the three numbers must increase in value – so 3, 29, 311 would be fine, as would 978, 979, 67,834. If you try this exercise with people you will almost always find that they quickly assume what the rule is and then check it by suggesting three numbers that conform to their rule. They keep getting positive responses but cannot find the rule. It is extremely rare for players to test their rule by deliberating suggesting three numbers that would break it, eg 10, 10, 10.

This mentality reflects our view of the world. We have a set of beliefs and assumptions and we look for evidence that bolsters this mindset. If we believe that all squirrels are grey then every time we see a grey squirrel it reinforces our conviction. But seeing another grey squirrel is a very poor test of the rule. What we should do is look to see if we can find a single squirrel that is not grey. That would disprove the rule and move our knowledge forward. The first reports that black swans had been seen in Australia were disbelieved in Europe – the evidence did not conform to the conventional view of the world so it was discounted.

Brilliant thinkers recognize that there are many different views of the world and that each is incomplete. Our current mindset frames how we view the world, but we must be ready to admit that it is just one of many views; it may be a good system, but it is partial and needs to be refreshed with new information. Sir Isaac Newton redefined our understanding of the world with his laws of gravity and motion. It was an excellent model and served science well for centuries until Albert Einstein updated it with his general theory of relativity. His view of the universe is constantly being examined and revised as new theories develop.

Einstein said, 'Imagination is more important than knowledge.' Divergent thinking allows us to use our imagination

to explore all sorts of new possibilities. Convergent thinking allows us to use our knowledge to examine concepts and see where they fit. Unfortunately our natural tendency is to reject ideas if they are not aligned with our existing knowledge and belief systems.

Divergent thinking involves considering all sorts of points of view – including the unconventional, the unfashionable, the ridiculous and the outlandish. It is an essential skill, which goes unpractised for many. There are times when we need the precision of convergent thinking and there are times when it is overly restrictive. The two main phases of a brainstorm meeting are good examples of how both methods can be employed in harmony. After the challenge has been defined, the group adopts a divergent thinking mode and generates a plethora of ideas. These will include many silly and unworkable notions, but these are useful as stimulants to provoke further ideas. When a good list has been assembled the facilitator of the brainstorm will encourage the group to start using convergent thinking in order to evaluate the ideas and to select the best. It is vital that the two modes of thinking are used separately in each phase. If we mix convergent thinking with divergent thinking at the beginning then ideas are evaluated and criticized as soon as they emerge, and the creative fountain will probably be extinguished.

The conventional thinker is normally stuck in convergent thinking mode, but the brilliant thinker can use both these modes. There are times when we need to be analytical, calculating, critical and judgemental, but if we use this approach too often then we become limited, constrained and even destructive in our thinking. We need to consider many possibilities, approach problems from different points of view and come at the problem laterally (literally from the side) if we are to be brilliant thinkers. We need to use divergent as well as convergent thinking. When Crick and Watson discovered the structure of DNA in Cambridge in 1953 they used divergent thinking to consider all sorts of possible patterns and arrangements. Then they used convergent thinking to narrow down to the one right answer – the double helix. When composers write an original piece of music they use divergent thinking to conceive innovative melodies and routes for the music to take. However, consciously or unconsciously, they use convergent thinking in structuring the piece with harmonies and chord sequences that are pleasing to the ear.

Convergent thinking is a useful tool, but it should not be the only method in our mental toolbox. If we can add imagination and divergent thinking then we can become more creative and multiply the effectiveness of our thinking many times.

2

Consider the opposite

In 1992 Rachel Nickell was brutally murdered on Wimbledon Common in London. The police brought in an expert, who constructed what he claimed was a psychological profile of the killer. The police found a suspect, Colin Stagg, who walked his dog on the Common and who fitted the profile. There was very little evidence that he had had anything to do with the crime, but the police became convinced that he was the murderer and they laid an elaborate 'honeypot' plan to encourage him to confess. This did not work, but they brought him to trial, where the judge threw the case out. Eventually, in 2008, Robert Knapper was convicted of the killing of Rachel Nickell. Knapper had been questioned in 1992 but wrongly eliminated. Stagg, who had spent 13 months in custody, was given a public apology and £706,000 in compensation. It is clear that once the police officers became convinced that Stagg was guilty they ignored contrary evidence and redoubled their efforts to build a case against him.

One of the most remarkable failings of human intelligence is the way that we cling to our beliefs and ignore contrary evidence. We have already mentioned the famous test run by Peter Wason. He repeated his experiment hundreds of times with different participants. It confirmed that people only suggested sequences that conformed with the pattern they had in mind. It was extremely rare for someone to do the more intelligent thing, which is to test a theory by trying something that breaks the rule they have in mind. When someone has a hypothesis he or she looks for evidence to support it and does not look for evidence that would disprove it.

Here is a slightly more sophisticated example. You are presented with four cards. You are told that each card has a number on one side and a letter on the other side. The four cards you see are as follows:

$$ E \quad 4 \quad 3 \quad J $$

You are asked to turn over the minimum number of cards that will help you determine if the following rule is true: any card with a vowel on one side will have an odd number on the other side. Which cards should you turn over? Take a moment to think about what you are trying to achieve here and which cards might help you to do it.

Most people would turn over the E and the 3. Their reasoning is as follows. If the E has an odd number on the other side and the 3 has a vowel on the other side then these are both examples that confirm the rule. This is true, but two instances that conform to the rule do not prove the rule.

Say we were driving on the motorway and I said, 'Drivers of sports car always exceed the speed limit.' The next two sports cars that we see are clearly exceeding the speed limit. Does that prove my statement to be universally true? Of course it does not. No matter how many sports cars we see speeding we need to see only one sauntering along in a sedate fashion to invalidate the rule. It is the same with the cards.

Turning over the E is helpful because it can disprove the rule. It does this if it has an even number on the reverse. The J is no use at all, as whatever it shows on the other side is irrelevant to the rule. The 3 is more interesting. It can support the rule if it shows a vowel but it cannot disprove the rule. If it shows a consonant on the reverse then this falls outside the rule and gives us no new evidence. The correct answer is that we should turn over the E (for the reasons given above) and the 4. If the 4 has a vowel on the other side then it disproves the rule.

The important point is that no number of supporting examples can prove a rule like this, but one example to the contrary can disprove it. To reiterate a famous case, consider the rule 'All swans are white.' If you lived in the northern hemisphere then you could spend a lifetime collecting thousands of instances that supported this rule. But one visit to Australia and the sight of a black swan would disprove it.

When the United States began escalating its military involvement in Vietnam, McGeorge Bundy, President Lyndon Johnson's special assistant for national security, was asked what would happen if the North Vietnamese responded by escalating their troop numbers in South Vietnam. 'We simply are not as pessimistic as you are,' Bundy responded. Pressed again he said, 'We just don't think that is going to happen.' The questioner then asked, 'But just suppose that it did occur?' Bundy refused to continue the conversation and ended it by saying, 'We can't assume what we don't believe.' If Bundy and others had been prepared to consider the opposite of what they believed then the United States might have been spared one if its worst national nightmares.[1]

In business, in our social lives and in many walks of life we construct hypotheses to explain situations. We constantly search for plausible explanations. Once we have one we tend to cling to it ferociously. We search for examples that will support it and we do not look for examples that would disprove it. The brilliant thinker knows that hypotheses are working models that are useful until proven wrong by a better hypothesis. Newton's laws of motion were excellent tools for centuries until Einstein came up with a more complete view of the universe. Similarly Einstein's theories are the best model we have until someone finds a flaw in them and comes up with something more fitting.

Francis Bacon said, 'The human understanding, when it has once adopted an opinion, draws all things else to support and agree with it. And though there be a greater number and weight of instances to be found on the other side, yet these it either neglects and despises, or else by some distinction sets aside and rejects.'

Stuart Sutherland gives five reasons why people are remarkably resistant to changing their beliefs:[2]

1. They consistently avoid exposing themselves to evidence that might disprove their beliefs.
2. On receiving such evidence they often refuse to believe it.
3. The existence of the belief distorts their interpretation of new evidence so as to make it consistent with the belief.
4. People selectively remember items that are in line with their beliefs.
5. People want to protect their self-esteem.

How do we go about considering the opposite? Quite simply, we have to suspend our belief set and ask the question 'What if?' What if every assumption we are making is wrong? What if what we believe to be true is not true? What if the opposite of what we believe were true? The brilliant thinker is uncomfortable with certainty. He or she is comfortable with ambiguity, with multiple possible explanations and with uncertainty.

NOTES

1. Charles McCoy (2002) *Why Didn't I Think of That?*, p 256, Prentice Hall, Paramus, NJ.
2. Stuart Sutherland (2007) *Irrationality*, p 109, Pinter & Martin, London.

3

Confront assumptions

Every time that we approach a problem, in any walk of life, we bring to bear assumptions that limit our ability to conceive fresh solutions. Brilliant thinkers are always aware of assumptions and are always happy to confront them.

There is a story told about a northern pike, a large carnivorous freshwater fish. A pike was put into an aquarium, which had a glass partition dividing it. In the other half from the pike there were many small fish. The pike tried repeatedly to eat the fish but each time hit the glass partition. The partition was eventually removed, but the pike did not attack the little fish. It had learnt that trying to eat the little fish was futile and painful so it stopped trying. We often suffer from this 'pike syndrome', where an early experience conditions us into wrong assumptions about similar but different situations.

Take a look at the picture. Study it for a moment and then decide what the builder replied to this complaint from the householder.

The way that we see things is often circumscribed by assumptions. In the Middle Ages the definition of astronomy was 'the study of how the heavenly bodies move around the

The extension you built for us is leaking. When can you fix it?

WHAT DOES THE BUILDER REPLY?

Earth'. The implicit belief was that the Earth was at the centre of the solar system. In 1510 a brilliant Polish astronomer, Nicolai Copernicus, postulated the idea that the Sun was the centre of the solar system and that all the planets revolved around the

Sun. He was able to explain the motions of the planets in a way that made sense but was totally at odds with convention. The atom was originally defined as the smallest indivisible unit of matter. The assumption was that an atom could never be subdivided. This belief hampered the advancement of science until eventually J J Thomson discovered the existence of a subatomic particle, the electron, in 1887.

In the 1930s the British and French military high commands assumed that any new war with Germany would be similar to the First World War, with huge static armies facing each other. The French built a massive defensive line along the entire border between France and Germany, the Maginot Line, consisting of enormous fortifications. But the Germans, when they attacked in May 1940, did some lateral thinking. They used fast-moving armoured divisions and paratroops. They swept through neutral Holland and Belgium and around the Maginot Line. The British and French were outmanoeuvred and France fell in five weeks. We see time and again from military history that assuming that new contests will be similar to previous ones is dangerous.

In business we make all sorts of assumptions. For example, you might hear people say:

■ 'Competition sets the price level in our industry.'
■ 'We must constantly raise our quality and service delivery.'
■ 'Our largest customers are our most important customers.'
■ 'We should hire people who fit in well with our team.'

Each of these notions needs to be challenged.

Often it is up to a newcomer to an industry to break the existing orthodoxies. For example:

■ Henry Ford challenged the assumption that automobiles were expensive hand-built carriages for the wealthy.

- Anita Roddick challenged the assumption that cosmetics had to be in expensive bottles. Her retail chain, Body Shop, sold products in plastic containers.
- IKEA challenged assumptions by allowing customers to collect their furniture from the warehouse.
- The low-cost airlines like Southwest and easyJet challenged the assumptions that you needed to issue tickets, allocate seats and sell through travel agents.
- Apple challenged the assumption that a personal computer was functional and not aesthetic.

Brilliant thinkers know that assumptions are there to be challenged and they relish defying them. How can you do this? Here are some tips:

- Start by recognizing that you, and everyone else, have ingrained assumptions about every situation.
- Ask plenty of basic questions in order to discover and challenge those assumptions.
- Write a list of all the ground rules and assumptions that apply in your environment and then go through the list and ask 'What would happen if we deliberately broke this rule?' 'What if we did the opposite of the norm?'
- Pretend you are a complete outsider and ask questions like 'Why do we do it this way at all?'
- Reduce a situation to its simplest components in order to take it out of your environment.
- Restate a problem in completely different terms.

Ken Olsen was CEO of DEC, which was a great innovator in the days of the minicomputer. He said, 'The best assumption to have is that any commonly held belief is wrong.'

How did you get on with the picture of the householder and the builder? The builder replied, 'I am sorry about that, sir, but I will take a look and get it fixed.' Did you assume that the builder was the man? Most people do.[1]

Just for fun, check your assumptions by quickly answering these 10 Wally Test questions.[2] They are mean, low questions and the only answer we can accept is the one given in Appendix 1.

1. How far can a dog run into a wood?
2. Which of the following animals would see best in total darkness: an owl, a leopard or an eagle?
3. Where are the kings and queens of Britain crowned?
4. If the vice-president of the United States were killed who would then become president?
5. Which candles burn longer – beeswax or tallow?
6. A farmer had four haystacks in one field and twice as many in each of his other two fields. He put the haystacks from all three fields together. How many haystacks did he now have?
7. If post is spelt POST and most is spelt MOST, how do you spell the word for what you put in the toaster?
8. A Muslim living in England cannot be buried on Church ground even if he converts to Christianity. Why not?
9. How many bananas can a grown man eat on an empty stomach?
10. What gets larger the more you take away?

The answers are in Appendix 1.

NOTES

1. From an idea in Guy Claxton (1998) *Hare Brain, Tortoise Mind*, Fourth Estate, London.
2. Taken from Paul Sloane and Des MacHale (1997) *Perplexing Lateral Thinking Puzzles*, Sterling Publishing, New York.

4

Analyse problems

The greatest challenge to any thinker is stating the problem in
a way that will allow a solution.

Bertrand Russell

Sometimes we face simple problems where it is easy to think of
and implement a good solution. Sometimes we face problems
that are large and complex. In this case it is generally better to
resist the temptation to launch in and take action. The serious
thinker prefers a more considered approach. Einstein said that
if he had one hour to save the world he would spend the first
55 minutes analysing the problem and then five minutes on
solutions. Why should we spend valuable time on analysis
when we could be out there tackling the issue? Here are some
of the benefits to be gained by investing in problem analysis:

- It stops you making premature judgements and jumping to
  the wrong conclusions.
- It challenges your assumptions.
- It gives you fresh insights into the real causes of the
  problem.
- It helps you to see connections between underlying
  causes.

- It can give you a sequence of items to tackle – a road map for solving the problem.
- It helps prioritize where you should put your efforts.

Furthermore if you do this as part of a team then it helps give everyone a common understanding of the underlying issues. If you do it with multiple teams then each team will approach the problem in a different way and generate different analyses, giving you fresh insights.

Here are some practical tools that you can use for problem analysis.

THE PATH TO THE IDEAL

Take three blank sheets of paper. On the first sheet list the current state of affairs with all the flaws, problems and difficulties you face. On the third sheet write the ideal state you would like to achieve with all problems solved and everything performing superbly – or however you care to define 'ideal'. Then on the top of the middle sheet write 'The Path'. Here you have to define the steps you need to take to get from where you are today to the ideal. The Path does not contain detailed solutions – this comes later. It simply lists the big magic solutions that you need. This method helps to define the problem and the key factors going forward. Each of the steps on the Path can now become a question that you can address using idea generation techniques.

WHY, WHY?

If you have children you will know that they often ask why and then when you give an answer they ask why again. It is an excellent method of increasing understanding, yet we do not do this as adults because we think it looks unsophisticated and childish. In this method we keep asking why. You write the problem on a large piece of paper and then ask why it happens (or happened). You list the major reasons and then for each of these you ask why. You can go down as many levels as you want until you have built as full a picture as possible of all the causes of the problem.

Say the problem was poor results from brainstorming meetings then the initial why, why? diagram might look like the one shown in Figure 4.1.

The process can be extended, for instance by asking why there was no confidence in the process or why there was a risk-averse culture.

The process can be extended to more levels. The why, why? method is easy to understand and yet potent. It works well for complex problems.

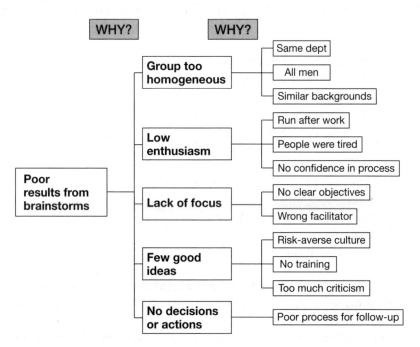

Figure 4.1 *Why, why? diagram*

SIX SERVING MEN

Six serving men is a problem analysis tool named after a poem by Rudyard Kipling:

> I keep six honest serving men, they taught me all I knew,
> Their names are What and Why and When and How and
> Where and Who.

You use the six words 'what', 'why', 'when', 'how', 'where' and 'who' to probe the issue. Each is used in a positive and negative context, giving effectively 12 questions to be addressed. List the problem and then ask each question in turn in a very literal way.

Let's say you are considering the complex problem of why some boys join criminal gangs. The questions you ask in turn could be as follows:

- What is good about gangs (from the boy's point of view)?
- What is bad about gangs?
- Why do gangs exist?
- Why do many boys not join gangs?
- When do boys join gangs?
- When do boys not join gangs?
- How do gangs recruit boys?
- How do boys resist or avoid gangs?
- Where do gangs operate?
- Where do gangs not operate?
- Who joins gangs?
- Who does not join gangs?

We ask each question in a very literal sense. So the 'where' question refers to actual places. The discipline of asking the 12 different questions in turn helps us to approach the problem from different angles. The method gives us some predictable or routine answers, but it will often turn up some unusual perspectives and insights. You can use it individually or in small groups with each group considering a smaller number of the questions.

LOTUS BLOSSOM

Lotus blossom is a rigorous problem analysis technique that originated in Japan. It is said to represent the peeling of the petals of a lotus blossom flower, where each petal reveals more petals underneath.

You write the problem inside a circle in the middle of a large piece of paper and then in a similar fashion to the why, why? method you identify what you think the main causes of the problem are. You choose the eight most important causes and write them in eight circles around the central circle.

Each of these eight causes becomes a theme in its own right and you have to find eight attributes, issues or causes for each. This results in nine sheets with each of the eight main themes generating a further eight sub-themes, as shown in Figure 4.2. So we end up with 64 issues, many of which are interrelated. It is best to start with a big table or wall for lotus blossom!

It may appear artificial and ponderous to go through this process in order to find 64 detailed causes, but that is the strength of the method. The discipline of examining the problem in this level of detail can generate insights and uncover connections that would otherwise be overlooked.

SUMMARY

Problem analysis techniques do not set out to solve the problem. They exist to help you to understand the underlying causes before attempting to find solutions. They assist you to see the overall nature of the problem and the interrelated causes. This in turn helps you to prioritize which areas to focus on. You can then generate many creative ideas for each problem, evaluate and select the best ideas and then build

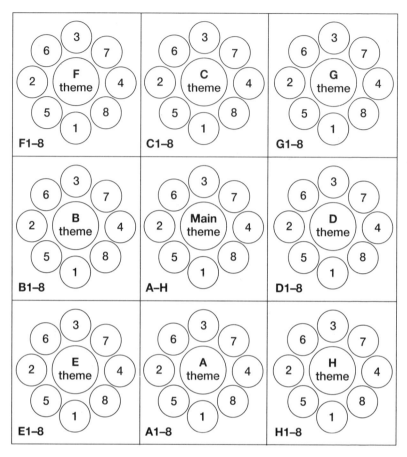

Figure 4.2 *Lotus blossom diagram*

a project plan for solving the problem. This is shown in the following sequence:

1. Define the problem.
2. Analyse the problem.
3. Prioritize the key problem components to solve.
4. Take each component in turn.
5. Generate many ideas.
6. Evaluate the ideas and select the best for implementation.
7. Develop a plan for implementation.

5

Ask questions

Children learn by asking questions. Students learn by asking questions. New recruits learn by asking questions. It is the simplest and most effective way of learning. People who think that they know it all no longer ask questions – why should they? Brilliant thinkers never stop asking questions, because they know that this is the best way to gain deeper insights.

Eric Schmidt, CEO of Google, said, 'We run this company on questions, not answers.' He knows that if you keep asking questions you can keep finding better answers.

When Greg Dyke became director-general of the BBC in 2000 he went to every major location and assembled the staff. They came expecting a long presentation. He simply sat down with them and asked a question, 'What is the one thing I should do to make things better for you?' Then he listened. He followed this with another question, 'What is the one thing I should do to make things better for our viewers and listeners?' He knew that at that early stage he could learn more from his employees than they could from him. The workers at the BBC had many wonderful ideas that they were keen to share. The fact that the new boss took time to question and then listen earned him enormous respect.

Columbo solves his mysteries by asking many questions, as do all the great detectives – in real life as well as fiction. All the

great inventors and scientists asked questions. Isaac Newton asked 'Why does an apple fall from a tree?' and 'Why does the Moon not fall into the Earth?' Charles Darwin asked 'Why do the Galapagos Islands have so many species not found elsewhere?' Albert Einstein asked 'What would the universe look like if I rode through it on a beam of light?' By asking these kinds of fundamental questions they were able to start the process that led to their tremendous breakthroughs.

The great philosophers spend their whole lives asking deep questions about the meaning of life, morality, truth and so on. We do not have to be quite so contemplative, but we should nonetheless ask the deep questions about the situations we face. It is the best way to get the information we need to make informed decisions.

If it is obvious that asking questions is such a powerful way of learning why do we stop asking questions? For some people the reason is that they are lazy. They assume they know all the main things they need to know and they do not bother to ask more. They cling to their beliefs and remain certain in their assumptions – yet they often end up looking foolish. Other people are afraid that by asking questions they will look weak, ignorant or unsure. They like to give the impression that they are decisive and in command of the relevant issues. They fear that asking questions might introduce uncertainty or show them in a poor light. In fact asking questions is a sign of strength and intelligence – not a sign of weakness or uncertainty. Great leaders constantly ask questions and are well aware that they do not have all the answers. Finally some people are in such a hurry to get on with things that they do not stop to ask questions because it might slow them down. They risk rushing headlong into the wrong actions.

At school, at home, in business and with our friends, family, colleagues, customers or managers we can check assumptions and gain a better appreciation of the issues by first asking questions. Start with very basic, broad questions; then move to more specific areas to clarify your understanding. Open questions are excellent – they give the other person or people a chance to give broad answers and they open up matters. Examples of open questions are:

- What business are we really in? What is our added value?
- Why do you think this has happened?
- What are all the things that might have caused this problem?
- How can we reduce customer complaints?
- Why do you think this person feels that way?
- What other possibilities should we consider?

As we listen carefully to the answers we formulate further questions. When someone gives an answer we can often ask 'Why?' The temptation is to plunge in with our opinions, responses, conclusions or proposals. The better approach is to keep asking questions to deepen our comprehension of the issues before making up our mind. Once we have mapped out the main points we can use closed questions to get specific information. Closed questions give the respondent a limited choice of responses – often just yes or no. Examples of closed questions are:

- When did this happen?
- Was the person angry?
- Where is the shipment right now?
- Did you authorize the payment?
- Would you like to go to the cinema with me on Saturday evening?

By giving the other person a limited choice of responses we get specific information and deliberately move the conversation forward in a particular direction.

In IBM sales training we were taught to respond to an objection with a question. The temptation is to rebut the objection immediately, but it is much better to ask one or more questions before contesting the issue. Let's say the client objects, 'Your proposal is too expensive.' The obvious thing to do is to tackle this head on: 'I think you will find that our proposal offers excellent value for money when you consider the benefits it offers.' However, a better approach is to ask a question: 'How do you mean, too expensive?' or 'Compared to what, can I ask?' By asking the other person to clarify the point you will learn more about the real nature of the objection. It also gives you time to construct a more accurate and better reply.

Asking many questions is very effective, but it can make you appear to be inquisitorial and intrusive. So it is important to ask questions in a friendly and unthreatening way. Do not ask accusing questions. 'What do you think happened?' will probably get a better response than 'Are you responsible for this disaster?' Try to pose each question in an innocent way and ensure that your body language is relaxed and amicable. Do not jab your finger or lean forward as you put your requests.

Try to practise asking more questions in your everyday conversations. Answer a question with a question. In a discussion, meeting or argument, the person asking the questions is the one controlling the agenda. So take control by enquiring. Instead of telling someone something, ask a question. Intelligent questions stimulate, provoke, inform and inspire. Brilliant thinkers never tire of asking questions. They are like children in their endless curiosity. They use questions to communicate, stimulate and understand. They know that questions help us to teach as well as to learn.

6

Think in combinations

Many great ideas are based on combining existing things in new and different ways. One of the greatest inventions of all time was the printing press, which was created by Johannes Gutenberg in 1440 in Strasbourg. He combined two existing ideas in order to develop a system of printing with movable type. He combined the flexibility of a coin punch with the power of a wine press. His invention transformed the spread of information in the Western world. It enabled the fast dissemination of books, pamphlets and papers on religious, political and scientific issues. It was the key technology that enabled the Reformation and the Renaissance – in just the same way that the internet has enabled the knowledge economy.

Two small ideas, the coin punch and the wine press, combined to make one mighty idea, the printing press. It was like the magic that occurred when humans first combined two soft metals, iron and tin, and created a strong alloy, bronze.

Great thinkers constantly look for new ways to combine things. What can we put with this idea to make something different? Not very long ago suitcases were just suitcases. You carried them or put them on a trolley. Then someone thought that it would be a good idea to combine the suitcase with the wheels from the trolley and came up with a suitcase with wheels. Now everyone wheels their suitcase. What are the wheels you can put on your 'suitcase'? What can you add to your product or service to make it better and easier for users? Rob Law took the idea one stage further. He combined a wheeled suitcase with a children's ride-on toy to invent the 'Trunki'. It featured on the UK TV programme *Dragons' Den*, where the experts ridiculed his idea and described it as worthless. It went on to be a big commercial success, with sales in 22 countries.

Trevor Baylis is the brilliant thinker who invented the clockwork radio. It appears to be an unlikely combination; radios need electricity, whereas clockwork is a mechanical method. Who would want to have their radio programmes interrupted and then have to go to the radio and wind it up? It is easier for us to use batteries or mains electricity. However, in many poor countries batteries are expensive and mains electricity is unreliable. Baylis overcame the doubters and built a reliable radio that people could wind up by hand. It has transformed the availability of information in many parts of the developing world.

You can use combinational thinking for products and services, but it also applies to other things such as partnerships. Who could you partner with to gain new skills or to access places or markets you cannot reach? Pavarotti performed with the Irish rock band U2. They came from two completely different musical genres; each brought a new audience to the other's music. When Mercedes-Benz wanted to build an innovative town car they collaborated not with another automobile company but with Swatch, a maker of fashion watches. Mercedes-Benz had the automobile engineering skills but they needed the design flair and lateral thinking of Swatch. Together they developed the Smart car.

Combining things is proven to be an excellent way of innovating. Many great new ideas are combinations of well-established ideas, just like the suitcase with wheels. Try forcing weird combinations and see what happens. For example, what would you get if you combined a school and a zoo? What possibilities does it suggest? Think about it for a minute and then see how your ideas compare with those below. You probably thought of many other novel concepts.

- Zookeepers could be invited to school to give lessons and show some of their animals.
- Children could be rewarded for attendance and good work with a trip to the zoo.
- A school could be located in a zoo. Why not?
- Each school could be allocated an endangered species that they studied and worked with a local zoo to help sustain.
- A school could collaborate with a zoo. Children could work after school as volunteers at the zoo and be rewarded with free passes for family and friends.

3M Corporation invented a glue that did not stick very well. It languished as a failure until Art Fry thought about combining it with a bookmark, which is something you want to stick and then move. The combination he developed became the Post-it note.

Abba Pater was the title of an audio CD produced by the Vatican in 1999. On it Pope John Paul II used something very close to a rap rhythm to convey some of his messages and prayers. Even an organization as conservative and well established as the Roman Catholic Church can find a weird combination to promote its message.

Develop the habit of thinking in combinations. When you see two products ask yourself how they could be combined. Someone may have seen a clock and a bell and created an alarm clock. Someone may have used an eraser and a pencil and thought 'Why not have a small eraser on the end of the pencil?' You can do the same – whether the items are used together or not, ask yourself the question 'How could they be combined?' When you meet people, if you discuss their business, imagine how your business and theirs might work together. If you discuss their hobbies ask how their interests and yours might be combined.

The next time you need a creative idea for a product, a service, a marketing message or anything else then try marrying two very different things and see what you come up with. It is one of the best-established ways of being truly creative.

7

Parallel thinking

Most of our thinking in the Western world is adversarial. It comes to us from an approach developed by the ancient Greeks. One person has a thesis and others test it with criticism. So, for example, when you propose an idea my natural reaction is to criticize it in order to test the strength of the idea. A good example of this model in operation is the prosecution and defence in a courtroom. The prosecutor brings forward all the evidence and arguments to show that the defendant is guilty and should be locked up. The defence lawyer disputes all these points and argues forcefully that the defendant should be found not guilty. Government and opposition parties in Parliament are also examples of adversarial thinking. The opposition party is obliged to oppose the government's policies and ideas. The trouble with this approach when we extend it to other walks of life is that adversarial thinking can make us entrenched, defensive and politicized. In meetings people dig into their own positions and do not acknowledge the advantages of their opponent's point of view. For example, the sales manager opposes an idea because it came from the marketing manager. Both parties then reinforce their positions. Another problem is that people can be inhibited from criticizing ideas that their boss puts forward. They do not want to be seen to be siding against the boss.

How can we overcome the limitations of adversarial thinking? One solution is to use parallel thinking, and the best-known tool for doing this is six thinking hats (STH). STH was created by Edward de Bono. It can be used in many situations, ranging from council meetings to jury rooms. It is particularly useful for evaluating innovative and provocative ideas. The six thinking hats technique overcomes the difficulties of adversarial thinking by forcing everyone to think in parallel. As each member of the group wears a particular hat he or she has to think a certain way. Here is how it would work in reviewing a proposal.

The proposal is read out and then everyone puts on the following hats in turn:

■ *The white hat*. This is the information hat. People can review or ask for more information or data to help analyse the proposal. There is no discussion of advantages or disadvantages – just a dispassionate review of the facts and data to hand.

■ *The red hat*. This hat represents emotions and feelings. People have to say how this proposal makes them feel emotionally. For example, some might say they feel threatened or scared by this idea. Others might say they feel encouraged or excited. It is important to get the feelings expressed, as they can be hidden reasons why people would oppose or support a proposal. 'It represents a poor return on investment' is a not a feeling – it is a rationalization, so it would not be allowed at this stage. 'I feel angry' or 'I feel happy' is the sort of response we want to draw out and record. The act of articulating feelings is cathartic. Once the feelings are out there we feel a sense of relief.

■ *The yellow hat*. This is the hat of sunshine and optimism. Everyone in turn has to say what is good about the proposal. Even if you think the idea stinks you have to find some redeeming qualities and good points about it. We list all the advantages and benefits from the success of the proposal. We can also prioritize them while wearing this hat.

▨ *The black hat* is the hat of pessimism. Everyone has to find fault with the idea. Even if it was your idea and you are very proud of it you have to point out some drawbacks and disadvantages. List all the possible ways it could go wrong. Point out the risks and dangers. Some people wear this hat all the time. We keep going until we can think of no more weaknesses. We can now prioritize the list – what are the biggest risks and drawbacks?

Before we put on the next hat, let's review what has happened here. We have reviewed the important facts and data. We have recorded everyone's initial feelings. We have listed and prioritized all the advantages of the proposal. We have listed and prioritized all the disadvantages. We have made enormous progress but we have not had any arguments or squabbling because the process has not allowed it. Of course we have to get to grips with the discussion – but this happens with the green hat on. We can now have a constructive discussion with all the pros and cons clearly laid out in front of us.

▨ *The green hat* is the hat of growth, creativity and possibilities. Everyone has to suggest ways in which the idea could be adapted or improved to make it work better. In what ways could we strengthen the benefits of the proposal? How can we mitigate the disadvantages? What ideas do people have to protect us against the risks we have identified? The green hat is the hat of brainstorming, of ideas, of evaluation and of negotiation. At this stage all sorts of possibilities exist. We could agree to the proposal or throw it out. We could agree an amended version of the proposal with some green hat improvements added. We could come up with a radically different idea that requires that we go back to the white hat and start the process again. At any stage we can put another hat on – provided that everyone wears the same-coloured hat at the same time.

▨ *The blue hat* is the process hat. It is used to check if the process is working well. When you wear it you discuss the method. You can use it at the start of the meeting to plan the process or at the end of the meeting to review what happened. If someone feels that the meeting is not working well that person can ask that everyone puts on the blue hat and discusses what is working and what is not.

Generally in meetings you will spend short amounts of time with the blue hat on. The group will spend some time with the white and red hats but most time with the yellow, black and green hats. You can go back and forth from one hat to another, but the key rule is that everyone must wear the same hat at the same time. Giving everyone a set of hats is very useful, because the action of physically changing hats helps to reinforce the change of thinking behaviour. It is good to have a chairperson who tells people to change hats or who holds up a coloured card or turns over a coloured cube to show which hat is in use and to make sure everyone is on board. So if the chairperson sees someone using black hat thinking during the yellow hat session that person must be brought back into line.

The method is simple to run and remarkably effective in all kinds of meetings. If you want to use this method then de Bono's book on the subject is highly recommended.[1]

While parallel thinking is usually seen as a group activity there is no reason why you cannot use it with two people or even on your own. Go through each of the hats in turn and be disciplined in approaching the issue with the mindset of the hat you are wearing. You will find that you gain a more rounded view of the problem.

NOTE

1. Edward de Bono (2000) *Six Thinking Hats*, 2nd edn, Penguin, London.

8

Think creatively
Great ways to boost your personal creativity

Brilliant thinkers are creative. They enjoy generating many ideas for any problem they face. But everyone gets stuck sometimes. Let's say you are wrestling with a tough issue – maybe at work, at home, with your children or in your social life. You have been working on this for a while and you can't seem to make a breakthrough. You want to come up with some really creative ideas. What can you do? Here are some practical ways to boost your inventiveness and help you crack the problem:

1. *Write down as many ideas as you can.* List routine ideas, creative ideas, silly ideas and so on. Initially aim for quantity. Try to write down 40, then 60 and then 80 ideas. Do not judge or reject ideas at this stage – just freewheel and brainstorm as many ideas as you can on your own. If you can persuade others to help then so much the better. When you have exhausted all the ideas you can conceive then go through and evaluate them using some broad criteria, eg is this idea feasible and would it be effective? Cross out the ineffective ideas, put one tick next to interesting ideas and

give two ticks to the really promising ideas. Now review your shortlist and decide which lines to pursue with some action.

2. *Draw a why, why? diagram.* Ask why the issue has arisen or why there is a problem. Write down several answers and then for each of these ask why again. Each answer becomes a question in its own right. At this stage you are not trying to solve the problem; you are trying to gain a deeper understanding of the possible causes of the problem. The why, why? diagram becomes a large mind map of the sources of the issue, and this can give you fresh insights and starting points for ideas for solutions.

3. *Talk it over with someone who has nothing to do with the situation.* This person will often ask basic questions or make seemingly silly suggestions that prompt good ideas. Two heads are better than one, but people who are too close to the issue will often come up with the same ideas as you, so try an outsider. For example, if it is a business issue then you might discuss it in general terms with a neighbour, a priest, a child, a sports coach, a writer, a musician, a grandmother, a teacher or a police officer. It is likely that the other person will come at the issue from a different perspective from yours.

4. *Ask how some celebrity would tackle the issue.* What would Barack Obama do? Or Steve Jobs? Or Napoleon, or Sir Richard Branson, or Salvador Dali, or Margaret Thatcher, or Madonna, or Sherlock Holmes? Choose forceful characters from fiction, from history or from today's TV news. Exaggerate this person's likely approach. Take it to its extremes and it will probably give you some radical solutions.

5. *Pick up any object at random and say to yourself, 'This item contains the key to solving the problem.'* Then force some ideas. Try this with several different objects and you will have a selection of radical and inventive ideas. Say your problem is finding time to write a book and the object you pick up is a beer bottle. Here are the sorts of ideas you might generate:

- Reward yourself with a bottle of beer every time you complete a section, or maybe a cup of tea for every page and a beer for every chapter and champagne when you complete the first full draft.
- Have a writer's party where you get some friends over to share a few drinks and contribute ideas.
- Leave a copy of the manuscript in the fridge. Then every time you open the fridge to get something to eat or drink you are reminded of the work that needs to be completed.
- Wherever you go, take some beer mats with you and write notes and ideas on them. If the beer mats are too bulky then try Post-it notes or just a notebook.
- The beer does not refresh anyone while it is in the bottle. It has to be poured out to be effective. The same applies to your ideas. They are no good left in your head – they have to be poured out.

6. *Use similes.* Try to think of a different problem in another walk of life that is like your problem. Say you want your staff at work to try new ways of working. You might imagine that this is like getting your children to eat vegetables. List various methods you might use with your children to encourage or persuade them to try vegetables. Then go through the list and see if any of the ideas can be converted into things you can try at work.

7. *Imagine an ideal solution in a world where there are no constraints,* eg you can use any resource you want. Now work back from that ideal and challenge each of the constraints that is holding you back from achieving it. Many of the obstacles can be overcome when you take this approach.

8. *Open a dictionary and take any noun at random.* Write down six attributes of that noun – so for 'tree' you might write 'root', 'branch', 'family', 'apple', 'trunk' and 'tall'. Then force some links between the word or its attributes and the problem in order to come up with fresh ideas. You will be surprised at how well this works – for individuals or in a group.

9. *Do something else.* Take a break. Go for a walk. Physical exercise increases oxygen flow to the brain and helps stimulate creativity. Sleep on the problem. Allowing the issue to incubate in your brain for a while seems to help your subconscious mind to put things into perspective and gather ideas. When you return to the issue after the break you will often have better ideas. Visit an art gallery or a museum. The range of external stimuli will help you conceive plenty of new ideas. Use the things you see as starting points to find new combinations and approaches. The artists who created the things you saw used all sorts of ways to communicate their message. Can you borrow any of their tactics?

10. *Draw a picture of the situation showing the people and the issues in simple cartoon style.* Put it up on the wall and then imagine how the story could develop. Think of it as a cartoon strip. Use Post-it notes to show different paths and possible consequences of actions. Many people's brains work better in images than in words or numbers, so this can lead to fantastic ideas. An example you may have seen is a TV detective programme where the police team put photos and clues on a large board and then use this as a way to explore leads to follow.

11. *Post a version of the problem on some internet blogs or bulletin boards and see what responses you get.* You can disguise the exact problem and post a hypothetical version that has the same principal problem. You can ask 'Has anyone faced this kind of issue and what did you do, please?' You may get silly answers, insulting answers or brilliant answers, so stay cool and revel in different points of view.

These methods work for individuals and for groups. Try them and see what suits you best. Above all, keep reminding yourself 'There are some great solutions for my problem. I haven't found the right one yet, but I will!'

9

Think laterally

Creative thinking involves conceiving something new. As such it is very broad and can include extensions of existing thoughts as well as radical new thoughts. Lateral thinking deliberately eschews conventional approaches and focuses on approaching the issue from fresh directions. All the classical painters were creative, but Picasso was lateral.

'Lateral thinking' is a phrase coined by Edward de Bono as a counterpoint to conventional or vertical thinking. In conventional thinking we go forward in a predictable, direct fashion. Lateral thinking involves coming at the problem from new directions – literally from the side. De Bono defines the four main aspects of lateral thinking as follows:

1. the recognition of dominant polarizing ideas;
2. the search for different ways of looking at things;
3. a relaxation of the rigid control of vertical thinking;
4. the use of chance.

There are dominant ideas in every walk of life. They are the assumptions, rules and conventions that underpin systems and influence people's thinking and attitudes. The idea that the Earth was flat and the idea that the Earth was the centre of the universe are examples of dominant ideas that polarized thought along set lines. Once the dominant ideas are in place then everything else is viewed in a way that supports them. People who are paranoid see every attempt to help them as malevolent and manipulating. Someone who believes in a conspiracy theory will explain away any inconvenient facts as deliberately constructed by the powers behind the conspiracy. Most organizations have dominant ideas that polarize their view of the world. It is easy for us to be critical of the makers of horse-drawn carriages who thought that automobiles were silly contraptions that would never catch on. However, we are the captives of established ideas too.

A lateral thinking technique we can use is to write down all the dominant ideas that apply in our situation and then deliberately challenge them. So, for example, the major airlines used to work with these beliefs:

- Customers want high standards of service.
- We issue tickets for all flights.
- We allocate seating in advance.
- We sell through travel agents.
- We fly to major airports because that is what business travellers want.

Of course, the low-cost airlines broke all of these rules and created a huge new market. A good start with lateral thinking is deliberately to turn every assumption and dominant idea on its head and see where that leads.

Asking 'What if?' is a lateral thinking technique that helps us to explore possibilities and challenge assumptions at the same time. We use the 'What if?' question to stretch every dimension of the issue. Each 'What if?' question should be extreme to the point of being ridiculous. Say we are running a small charity that cares for homeless dogs. The challenge is: 'How can we double our fund-raising income?' The sort of 'What if?' questions we could ask might be:

- What if we had only one donor?
- What if we had 10 million donors?

- What if we had an unlimited marketing budget?
- What if we had no marketing budget?
- What if everyone had to look after a homeless dog for a day?
- What if dogs slept in beds and people slept in kennels?
- What if dogs could speak?

The question 'What if we had only one donor?' might suggest that we target fabulously wealthy dog lovers in order to raise more funds from fewer donors. We could explore ways of doing this and generate all sorts of ideas. 'What if dogs could speak?' might suggest ways of marketing that involved speaking dogs or dog conversations. Each question generates stimulating lines of enquiry by testing the rules and dominant ideas boundaries that are assumed to apply to the problem. Start with a challenge and, individually or in a group, generate a shortlist of really provocative 'What if?' questions. Take one and see where it leads. Follow the crazy train of thought and see what emerges. You will start with silly ideas, but these often lead to radical insights and innovations.

The role of chance in major inventions and scientific discoveries is well documented. The transmission of radio waves was discovered by Hertz when some of his equipment happened to produce a spark on the other side of the room. Alexander Fleming discovered penicillin when he noticed that one of his old Petri dishes had developed a mould that was resistant to bacteria. X-rays were discovered accidentally by Roentgen when he was playing with a cathode ray tube. Christopher Columbus discovered America when he was looking for a route to India. The common theme is that someone with a curious mind sets out to investigate things. When something unusual happens the person studies it and sees how it can be put to use. The same methods can work for us. When we are looking for new ideas and fresh ways to do things then a random input can help us. A highly effective brainstorming technique is to take a noun at random from the dictionary. Write down some associations or attributes of the word and then force-fit connections between the word or its associations and the brainstorming challenge. People do not believe that it works until they try it. Some words produce nothing worthwhile but every so often you will get really radical ideas using this method. The same approach works using a random object, picture, song and so on. This is why a walk around a museum or art gallery can be so useful when we are working on a knotty problem. The brain can make all sorts of lateral connections between the variety of stimuli that you encounter and the problem.

Lateral thinking puzzles are strange situations where you are given a small amount of information and then have to try to figure out what is going on by asking questions. They work best as a group game. One person acts as quizmaster. Others fire in questions. The quizmaster can answer only 'Yes', 'No' or 'Irrelevant'. The puzzles are great fun and at the same time they teach techniques for questioning, testing assumptions, using your imagination and piecing together clues. When you get stuck you have to come at the problem from new directions – which is where the lateral thinking comes in.

Probably the best-known puzzle is the man in the elevator. A man lives on the tenth floor of a building. Every day he takes the elevator to go down to the ground floor to go to work or to go shopping. When he returns he takes the elevator to the seventh floor and walks up the stairs to reach his apartment on the tenth floor. He hates walking so why does he do it?[1]

If you do not already know the answer you can find it in Appendix 1.

A great deal of humour is based on lateral thinking. Comedians ridicule existing beliefs; they come at an issue from unusual directions; they make unexpected connections to give the surprise that makes us laugh. The two best reasons to use lateral thinking in our everyday lives are because we will generate many fresh, better ideas and because it is great fun.

NOTE

1. From Paul Sloane (1991) *Lateral Thinking Puzzlers*, Sterling Publishing, New York.

10

Think what no one else thinks

How can you think of things that no one else thinks of? The answer is by deliberately taking a different approach to the issue from everyone else. As pointed out in Chapter 9 on lateral thinking, there are dominant ideas in every field. The brilliant thinker purposefully challenges those dominant ideas in order to think innovatively.

Albert Szent-Gyorgyi, who discovered Vitamin C, said, 'Genius is seeing what everyone else sees and thinking what no one else has thought.' If you can identify the standard viewpoint and then survey the situation from a different viewpoint you have an excellent chance of gaining a new insight. When Jonas Salk was asked how he invented the vaccine for polio he replied, 'I imagined myself as a virus or cancer cell and tried to sense what it would be like.'

Ford Motor Corporation asked Edward de Bono, who originated the concept of lateral thinking, for some advice on how they could clearly differentiate themselves from their many competitors in car manufacturing. De Bono gave them a very innovative idea. Ford had approached the problem of competing from the point of view of a car manufacturer and asked the question 'How can we make our cars more attractive to consumers?' De Bono approached the problem from another direction and asked the question 'How can we make the whole driving experience better for Ford customers?' His advice was that Ford should buy up car parks in all the major city centres and make them available for Ford cars only. His remarkable idea was too radical for Ford, which saw itself as an automobile manufacturer with no interest in the car parks business.

In 1954 the British government held an auction for commercial television regions. Many companies were interested in bidding for the franchises. They analysed the demographics of the regions to identify which were the wealthiest regions that would produce the most advertising revenues. The result was that they focused on London and the South-East of England. Sydney Bernstein was managing director of a small chain of cinemas, Granada Cinemas. He wanted to compete in the auction. He told his people, 'Don't look for the richest region; look for the wettest. Find me the region with highest rainfall.' This turned out to be the North-West of England. Granada bid for this and won it. Bernstein's idea was that it was better to have a region where it rained so much that people stayed in and watched TV. He succeeded by approaching the problem from a different point of view. He thought what no one else thought. Granada went on to produce many innovative programmes, including *Coronation Street* and *World in Action*.

The spectators at the Olympic Games in Mexico City in 1968 were amazed to see a young athlete perform a high jump with his back to the bar. Until then, every high jumper 'rolled' over the bar with his or her face down. Dick Fosbury, an American, introduced an entirely new approach, the 'flop', leaping over with his back close to the bar and his face up. Fosbury was ranked 48th in the world in 1967; yet in 1968 he caused a sensation when he won the Olympic gold medal with his unprecedented technique and a leap of 2.24 metres. What he introduced was a leap of the imagination – and it revolutionized high jumping. Nowadays all the top jumpers use his method. He thought what no one else thought and conceived a new method.

How can we force ourselves to take a different view of a situation? Instead of looking at the scene from your view, try looking at it from the perspective of a customer, a product, a supplier, a child, an alien, a lunatic, a comedian, a dictator, an anarchist, an architect, Salvador Dali, Leonardo da Vinci and so on. Apply the 'What if?' technique described in Chapter 9. Challenge all the common assumptions. If everyone else is looking for the richest region, look for the wettest. If everyone else is facing the bar then turn your back on it.

If you had to study a valley, how many ways could you look at it? You could look up and down the valley; you could scan it from the riverside or stand and look across it from each hillside. You could walk it, drive along the road or take a boat down the river. You could study a satellite photo. You could peruse a map. Each gives you a different view of the valley and each adds to your understanding of the valley. Why not do the same with any problem? Why do we immediately try to frame a solution before we have approached the problem from multiple differing perspectives?

The great geniuses did not take the traditional view and develop existing ideas. They took an entirely different view and transformed society. Picasso took a different view of painting; he saw cubes, shapes and impressions instead of accurate images. Einstein imagined a new approach to physics: a world where time and space were relative. Darwin conceived a different view of the origin of species; he saw how they might have evolved rather than been created. Each of them looked at the world in a new way. In similar fashion Jeff Bezos took a different view of book retailing with Amazon.com, Stelios Haji-Ioannou took a new perspective on flying with easyJet, Swatch transformed our view of watches and IKEA changed the way we buy furniture. If we can attack problems from entirely new directions then we can think of things that conventional thinkers miss. It gives us unlimited possibilities for innovation.

11

Evaluate ideas

Generating a large number of ideas is a key part of the creative thinking process. The more ideas you come up with the more likely you are to find something truly innovative. But having a long list of ideas creates an issue. How do you select the best ideas to carry through to implementation?

Have you ever been in a brainstorm session where you filled flip charts with ideas and then the manager said 'Thanks very much; leave those with me and I will analyse them later' and you never heard anything again? The ideas on their own are just the starting point. Without proper evaluation there will be no follow-through to completion.

When it comes to innovation, the evaluation phase of the process is critical to the success of the session and typically needs as much time and attention as the idea generation stage. In evaluation we switch from suspending judgement to exercising critical judgement in order to whittle down the ideas to a shortlist of actionable items.

SELECTION CRITERIA

How do you evaluate the ideas? By setting some selection criteria. The criteria should be reasonably broad but not

vague. 'We are looking for good ideas' is too fuzzy – all sorts of things can get through. 'We want ideas we can implement immediately with no extra resource' is almost certainly too tight and will result in good ideas being rejected.

Say you were analysing ideas for new products. The criteria you agree might well be:

- Will customers like it?
- Is it technically feasible?
- Will it make money?

Each idea is then assessed against these measures. It is best to have a short list of broad conceptual criteria rather than a long list of detailed rules.

A recommended general set of criteria for all sorts of ideas is the FAN method from Synectics. Are you a FAN of the idea?

That is:

- Is it feasible?
- Is it attractive?
- Is it novel?

The third criterion here is important to ensure that fresh ideas are valued highly.

The British retail giant Tesco uses the following criteria for selecting ideas in brainstorms or suggestions sessions:

- Is it better (for customers)?
- Is it simpler (for staff)?
- Is it cheaper (for Tesco)?

Any idea that is better, easier and cheaper is likely to be a good idea and will probably be approved. Putting the criteria into context – eg simpler for staff – makes it easier to understand and apply.

Choose the criteria you want and then apply them rigorously to the ideas on your list. If in doubt try 'feasible, attractive, novel' or 'better, simpler, cheaper' and see how well they work for you.

TRIAGE

Another quick way to cut down a long list of ideas is to perform a triage. Each idea is flagged as belonging to one of three categories based on the selection criteria you have agreed:

- It won't fly and gets crossed out.
- It looks interesting and gets one tick.
- It looks a great idea and gets two ticks.

A second pass of the triage may be needed to sort out the questionable ideas. The act of putting each idea into one of three boxes based on clear criteria is simple but effective. It quickly eliminates the least useful ideas and helps you to focus on and select the very best.

GROUP EVALUATION METHODS

If you are working in a group and have a long list of ideas to evaluate then the usual method is for the facilitator to go through each item and canvass opinions or perform a triage as described above. This can be a long-winded process, so here are some alternative methods:

- Each person is given five 'ticks' they can spend. They come to the front and put ticks next to their favourite ideas. The ideas with the most ticks go forward. This method is quick and energetic but it does mean that some of the more obscure ideas may be overlooked. Their potential may be developed if they are discussed. Another possible drawback is that in controversial or political situations people can be inhibited or influenced by the opinions of others.
- There is a secret ballot and people write on slips of paper their favourite ideas. This overcomes the problem of political correctness where people may be afraid to support controversial ideas or may be influenced by the more powerful voices in the room. There is no discussion during the ballot but once the ideas are ranked the group discussion can begin.
- Each person in turn states their favourite idea. The facilitator goes around the room and gives everyone the opportunity to speak. This is quick and interactive but it means that the people who speak later can be unduly influenced by what has gone before.

Whether you are working on your own or in a group, sound evaluation of ideas is an invaluable part of the process. It is important to remember to separate the two types of thinking used in the two stages of the process. We use divergent thinking while generating ideas. We suspend judgement and generate a long list of ideas, including silly and unreasonable ideas. We do not limit ourselves at this stage. We use one idea to trigger another. When we have enough ideas or when we have exhausted our creative process then we use convergent thinking to select the best ideas. We can now be critical and analytical. We compare the ideas against clear criteria and make judgements as to which will succeed and which will not. Many people mix the two methods and apply convergent thinking to eliminate lines of enquiry as they go along. This is fatal; many potentially fruitful ideas will be killed at birth. Stay divergent in idea generation and use convergent thinking only when you move to the evaluation phase.

12

Make difficult decisions

From time to time we are faced with difficult choices between several options each of which has attractions and disadvantages. For example, this could happen when we are choosing a new home and have seen a number of appealing houses none of which is absolutely ideal. In business we may have to choose between competing new product ideas or new markets. We have to select one choice among many. The approach that is commonly used is to consider the pros and cons of each option, argue and discuss for a little while, and then make a decision based on our feelings and intuition. We tend to use some analytics in considering the options but then go 'with our gut' when it comes to the final decision. The trouble is that our choice is subjective and therefore open to criticism. How can we be sure that we made the right choice when ultimately it was based on our feelings rather than anything rigorous? Did we make a rational decision or was it overly influenced by our mood and emotions on that day? If our decision is criticized then we will probably defend it vigorously and try to convince ourselves and others that there were many good reasons for it.

Important decisions need more than instinct. A generalized method for making major decisions consists of the following elements:

1. Analyse the problem. Gather data from various sources. Use the techniques shown in Chapter 4, 'Analyse problems'. Try to understand what is causing the problem. Break it into manageable chunks.
2. Generate many ideas using creative thinking techniques. See Chapter 8, 'Think creatively'.
3. Evaluate the ideas to come up with a shortlist.
4. List the pros and cons of different courses of action.
5. If time allows then sleep on it. Let the decision incubate for a little while.
6. Make the decision.
7. Review the decision down the line – and be prepared to change your mind if it proves that you made the wrong choice.

Some significant decisions demand an even more precise approach. Say, for example, you are considering whether to close an old factory and replace it with a new one on the same site, replace it with a new unit at one of two lower-cost locations or outsource the activity to a third party in India or China. You have seven separate options:

1. Retain and refurbish the existing factory.
2. Build a new factory on the existing site.
3. Buy a new factory in location A.
4. Buy a new factory in location B.
5. Outsource to Company X in India.
6. Outsource to Company Y in China.
7. Do nothing.

How would most senior management teams approach this kind of decision? They would gather data on each of the options. They might appoint a small committee to study the options in depth and make a recommendation. Then the whole team might consider the recommendation and either accept or reject it. The problem is that very often emotion and politics cloud the issue and influence the outcome. A more rigorous approach would be to use a weighted pair ranking matrix to analyse the choices.

Let's see how this method works. First we list all the options as above. Second we list all the criteria that we will use to make the decision. The criteria might be:

A. ongoing manufacturing cost (minimize);
B. cost of the change (minimize);
C. disruption costs and time of changeover (minimize);
D. flexibility to cope with peaks and troughs of demand (maximize);
E. availability of skilled and unskilled labour (maximize);
F. loss of skills and experience (minimize);
G. confidence in the quality of output (maximize);
H. risk of failure, disruption or discontinuity (minimize).

Some of these criteria are in conflict and we need to prioritize them. We might do this with a discussion leading to some kind of consensus on the ranking order. However, for something this important it is better to use a rigorous method to allocate the ranking weights to the criteria.

PAIR RANKINGS

Pair ranking is a method whereby each option is compared with each other option in a binary choice. At each stage the preferred option is given one mark and then we move on to the next pair. So in our example we would compare option A, the ongoing manufacturing cost, with option B, the cost of the changeover. If it was agreed that option A was more important then it would get one vote and option B would get none. We then compare option A with option C and choose which of these is more important. There are eight criteria so we compare option A with the other seven one at a time. We then do the same for option B. It has already been compared to option A, so we compare it against option C and choose our preference and then compare it to option D and so on. For eight options we will need to make 28 binary choices. (The formula is N × (N−1)/2). This may seem tedious but it is an absolutely essential part of the process. It is much easier to make a rational decision when comparing two options. If we try to rank all eight in order of importance without first doing the pair comparisons then we risk making a subjective and inaccurate choice.

Let's suppose that after doing the pair comparisons we arrive at these numbers of marks:

A. Ongoing manufacturing cost (minimize)   7
B. Cost of the change (minimize)   2
C. Disruption costs and time of changeover (minimize)   1
D. Flexibility to cope with peaks and troughs of demand
   (maximize)   6
E. Availability of skilled and unskilled labour (maximize)   5
F. Loss of skills and experience (minimize)   0
G. Confidence in quality of output (maximize)   3
H. Risk of failure, disruption or discontinuity (minimize)   4

We now have a clear priority for our criteria and we can give each of the criteria a weighting in line with its priority. Initially we assign option A 7 out of 28 = 25 per cent and so on:

A. Ongoing manufacturing cost (minimize)   25%
B. Cost of the change (minimize)   7%
C. Disruption costs and time of changeover (minimize)   4%
D. Flexibility to cope with peaks and troughs of
   demand (maximize)   21%
E. Availability of skilled and unskilled labour
   (maximize)   18%
F. Loss of skills and experience (minimize)   0%

G. Confidence in quality of output (maximize)   11%
H. Risk of failure, disruption or discontinuity
   (minimize)   14%

We can go with these percentage weightings or we can discuss and then adjust them, but keeping the same order. After discussion we might arrive at the following:

A. Ongoing manufacturing cost (minimize)   23%
B. Cost of the change (minimize)   7%
C. Disruption costs and time of changeover (minimize)   5%
D. Flexibility to cope with peaks and troughs of
   demand (maximize)   20%
E. Availability of skilled and unskilled labour
   (maximize)   18%
F. Loss of skills and experience (minimize)   2%
G. Confidence in quality of output (maximize)   12%
H. Risk of failure, disruption or discontinuity
   (minimize)   13%

We can now construct our decision matrix, with the options down the side and the criteria across the top:

		A	D	E	H	G	B	C	F	Total
		Mfg cost	Flexibility	Labour	Risk	Quality	Cost	Disruption	Loss skills	
		23%	20%	18%	13%	12%	7%	5%	2%	
1	Refurbish existing									
2	New on same site									
3	Location A									
4	Location B									
5	India									
6	China									
7	Do nothing									

We now go through the pair rating system for each pair of options for each criterion. So we start with the first column and compare option 1 against option 2 just on the basis of the ongoing manufacturing costs. A new factory on the same site could be built to a more efficient design so it wins this comparison and gets a mark. We then compare option 1 against option 3 and give one mark to the winner. We carry on doing this for each pair of options and for each of the criteria. This is a time-consuming process, but the low-level and precise nature of the comparisons means that we can have confidence in the overall result. Let's suppose that after the pair rankings we get the following scores in each column:

		A	D	E	H	G	B	C	F	Total
		Mfg cost	Flexibility	Labour	Risk	Quality	Cost	Disrup-tion	Loss skills	
		23%	20%	18%	13%	12%	7%	5%	2%	
1	Refurbish existing	1	1	0	5	4	5	5	5	
2	New on same site	3	4	2	4	5	0	0	4	
3	Location A	4	5	3	3	3	1	4	3	
4	Location B	2	6	6	2	6	2	1	2	
5	India	5	2	5	0	1	3	2	1	
6	China	6	3	4	1	2	4	3	0	
7	Do nothing	0	0	1	6	0	6	6	6	

We now apply the percentage weightings to each of the marks to get the weighted marks shown as percentages and total for each option:

	A	D	E	H	G	B	C	F	Total
	Mfg cost	Flexibility	Labour	Risk	Quality	Cost	Disruption	Loss skills	
	23%	20%	18%	13%	12%	7%	5%	2%	
1 Refurbish existing	23	20	0	65	48	35	25	10	226
2 New on same site	69	80	36	52	60	0	0	8	305
3 Location A	92	100	54	39	36	7	20	6	354
4 Location B	46	120	108	26	72	14	5	4	395
5 India	115	40	90	0	12	21	10	2	290
6 China	138	60	72	13	24	28	15	0	350
7 Do nothing	0	0	18	78	0	42	30	12	180

This shows that a new factory at Location B is the best choice. If someone complains that it fails on the most important criterion – manufacturing costs – then we can show that it is the number one choice for flexibility, labour availability and quality and that these factors outweigh the disadvantage on cost. Incidentally the default option of doing nothing was the best option for minimizing risk, disruption and potential loss of skills but it still came last because of the weighting of the decision criteria.

Brilliant thinkers know when to use the left brain for analytical and logical thinking, critical analysis and convergent thinking. They also know when to use the right side of the brain for creativity, ideas, intuition and divergent thinking. When it comes to important decisions we should be wary of trusting our instincts. We should go through a critical and impartial analysis using a tool such as a weighted pair ranking. If we feel unhappy about the outcome then we must go back and check all the assumptions that led to it. If necessary we can repeat the process. You can generally trust it to give you the best result.

Once you have arrived at the best decision and thought through the consequences it is time to take action and to implement your choice.

13

Develop your verbal thinking

The most common method of thinking in the Western world is verbal thinking. Although we have a range of intelligences including numerical, musical, spatial, emotional, verbal and kinaesthetic intelligences it is the verbal one that we depend on most. We tend to think and express ourselves in words. It can be argued that verbal intelligence, ie mastering the use of words, is the most important skill we develop because acquiring further skills depends on our comprehension of language. A tremendous proportion of the early learning for an infant is in developing verbal skills – learning to speak, to understand speech, to read and to write. Whether a baby is brought up in Beijing, Madrid, Sydney or Moscow it will surely spend thousands of hours acquiring expertise in its native language. He or she will become proficient with the amazing range, power, complexity and sophisticated subtleties of language. However, once a certain competence has been acquired most people stop developing verbal skills.

Studies have shown that there is a strong correlation between people's abilities with words and range of vocabulary and success in their chosen fields. People who can express

themselves clearly are perceived as more intelligent and of higher status. They are accorded greater respect. So why do we not continue to enhance our verbal skills? Why do we stop doing what we spent most of our early years doing? The trouble is that we take our verbal abilities for granted. Once we have mastered reading, writing and speaking we move on to other things. We have acquired the most important tool in our mental toolbox. We depend on it for all sorts of tasks but we rarely take time to sharpen it. It makes better sense to maintain, enhance and extend the tool. Here are some ways we can do that.

GET A GOOD DICTIONARY AND THESAURUS

Two of the most loyal companions on your desk should be a dictionary and a thesaurus. Use the dictionary to learn the meanings and derivations of new words you encounter. Also use it to check the exact meanings and spellings of words that you are unsure of. The thesaurus is very helpful whenever you are writing and need an alternative to a word in order to avoid repetition or to achieve a variation in meaning. Your computer probably offers a spellchecker and a thesaurus so by all means use them. They can be handy digital aids to be used alongside the mighty physical volumes.

READ

It may seem silly to advise people who are reading this text that they should read but in the modern world we are so busy with work and we are bombarded with so much information by TV broadcast, telephone and the internet that reading books and articles can be squeezed out of our agenda. Reading the works of really good writers is one of the best ways to develop our abilities with words. Modern and classic novels, leading non-fiction books and top-quality newspaper and magazine articles are all important sources for us. How often do you find time to read poetry? Try some new poems and reread old favourites for inspiration and appreciation of the sublime skills of the poet. Reading works that are well written helps at two levels. It will increase our understanding of concepts and our acquisition of knowledge and at the same time it helps develop our core skills at comprehension, vocabulary and expression. Most of our reading should be speed reading so that we are taking in the information rapidly. There are various books and courses on speed reading. However, when we occasionally encounter a piece of text that is extremely cogent or well written we should reread it, taking time to examine what it is that makes it so successful. We should savour the words and metaphors that the author uses, analyse his or her arguments, underline the key points and perhaps make a note to mimic some of this style in our own writing.

If you are fortunate enough to have a partner who likes reading then try reading aloud to each other. Choose an interesting short piece and read it for your partner with feeling and emphasis. Children learn by listening to their parents or teachers read and by reading to them. We can do the same and it should be a pleasurable activity. When you have read the piece you can discuss it with your partner. What did each of you get out of it? What aspects of the author's style did you like most? What points did the author make and do you agree with them? Play at being students again.

CAPTURE NEW WORDS

There is a regular feature in the *Reader's Digest* magazine entitled 'It pays to expand your word power'. It is sound advice. Whenever we bump into new words we should turn to the dictionary and spend a moment learning the meaning and derivation of the word. It is easy to skip new words and race on through the text, so we need discipline if we are not to lose this opportunity. Say we come across the word 'philology'. It means the science of language and its historical development. It comes from the ancient Greek word *philos*, meaning 'a friend', and the Greek word *logos*, meaning 'a word' – so philology's roots mean 'love of words'. While we are in this section of the dictionary we might notice that 'philanthropy', 'philately', 'philharmonic' and 'philosophy' all use the same Greek root of *philos* and they all refer to the love of something. If we do this we are on our way to becoming philologists, people who love words and study the science of language.

As you build your vocabulary you should try to use the new words in context, as this helps you to remember them. However, it can look pompous or pretentious to use many long and obscure words in everyday speech. The main benefit of having a large vocabulary is the ability to use a word with exactly the right meaning at a time when it is appropriate. A secondary benefit is that we better understand intellectual writing. There are many guides to good writing style and you have to find one that suits you. In general it is better to keep your written and spoken sentences short and clear. But do not hesitate to use an unusual word occasionally when it conveys exactly the meaning you require.

WRITE, REWRITE AND EDIT

We all write, whether it is a text message on a mobile phone, an e-mail message or a novel, and we can all improve our writing. A good way to improve your writing is to read over what you have written and ask yourself these questions:

- Does what I have written express exactly what I mean?
- Will it be clear and comprehensible to the reader?
- Can I make it more concise or more accurate?

We should look for superfluous words and sentences. Most of our digital photographs can be improved by cropping in order to focus on the subject. In exactly the same way, most of our written work can be improved by cutting out unnecessary or repetitive elements.

PLAY WITH WORDS

Children learn language by playing with words, testing, experimenting, making mistakes and being gently corrected. We should adopt a playful attitude towards words and treat them as friends. Word games will increase your verbal dexterity and intelligence rating. Many standard IQ tests use word puzzles. Anagrams, cryptic crosswords, code-breakers, word searches, dingbats (also known as rebuses) and other verbal conundrums are excellent mental exercise. Scrabble is ideal in this regard. If you want to play it seriously you will have to learn many obscure short words that use the high-value letters. The dictionary game is simple but fun. One person reads out a definition from the dictionary and others have to identify the word. The reader can choose a common word but start with one of its less common meanings.

Practice improves your performance with word puzzles, which is one reason why people can prepare for IQ tests and improve their scores in them.

LISTEN TO YOURSELF

In just the same way that you critically review your draft writing in order to sharpen it you should try to do the same with your speech. If it is possible, view some video clips of yourself speaking. This is particularly useful if you are rehearsing for an important talk or presentation. Most people are surprised to discover that they display a number of errors or bad habits in their everyday speech. For example, many people pepper their talk with filler words or phrases such as 'like', 'well' or 'you know'. Hesitation, repetition, rambling and mumbling are other common faults.

Rudyard Kipling wrote, 'Words are the most powerful drug used by mankind.' They can paint amazing images, inspire and intoxicate. If you continually work on developing your range of words and skills with words then you will reap the rewards.

Take the verbal intelligence questionnaire

1. Whenever I come across a word that is new to me, I check its meaning and derivation in the dictionary.
2. I enjoy reading books.
3. I find time for reading books or articles most days.
4. I discuss books and their meanings with other people.
5. I like to learn new words and to use them.
6. I check what I write to ensure that it is clear.
7. I like to make my writing concise, so I deliberately eliminate unnecessary or repetitive words or sentences.

8. I enjoy word puzzles such as crosswords.
9. I sometimes play word games such as Scrabble.
10. I feel confident that I can express myself clearly and I am rarely lost for words.

Score one point for every positive (yes) answer. A score of 8 out of 10 is good.

14

Think mathematically

As you go through life you meet people who tell you that they never liked mathematics. They are frightened or wary of mathematical concepts. They are clumsy with numbers and struggle or avoid issues of variables, means, probabilities, graphs or statistics in anything more than a simple form. You should feel sorry for these people. They will be at a severe disadvantage in business, where it is immensely helpful to have a good grasp of numbers, arithmetic and percentages as well as an understanding of concepts like proportionality and dependent variables. The mathematically innumerate are not only restricted in the thinking tools that they can use, but also denied an appreciation of the power and beauty of mathematics.

Most of our thinking is verbal thinking. We think in terms of words, verbal concepts and verbal reasoning. We apply some logic. But there are some problems for which words and logic are poor tools. Try this problem:

The farmer. A farmer sells 10 tons of potatoes every year. He also grows enough seed potatoes for next year's planting. If his yield is

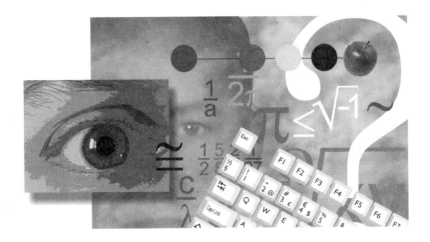

exactly 20 times what he sows how many tons of potatoes does he need to plant to ensure a perpetual supply?[1]

How would you go about solving this problem? Try it for a while and see how you get on. Here is another puzzle, which is fairly straightforward. Please take a break and try to solve it and then we will look at how you approached the task.

The journey. I drove to Birmingham early one morning at an average speed of 60 miles per hour. I drove back in the afternoon at an average speed of 40 miles per hour. What was my average speed for the combined journey?

The first problem, the farmer, can be approached in different ways, but it is a little tricky to solve unless you use algebra, in which case it becomes very straightforward. Let x be the weight of the seed potatoes he plants each year. Then we know that:

$$20x = 10 + x$$
$$\text{so } 19x = 10$$
$$x = 10/19 \text{ tons} = 0.526 \text{ tons}$$

Algebra is ideal when we have some unknowns and some facts about them that we can express as equations. We can use it in all sorts of ways, including helping us with numerical problems. If one square room has 1,000 tiles by 1,000 tiles and a second square room has 1,003 tiles by 1,003 tiles then how many more tiles are there in the second room than in the first? How much more is 1,003 squared than 1,000 squared? We can use:

$$a^2 - b^2 = (a + b) \times (a - b)$$

where a is 1,003 and b is 1,000

so the answer is

$$(1,003 + 1,000) \times (1,003 - 1,000) = 2,003 \times 3 = 6,009$$

What was your answer for the journey? Most people would say rather automatically that the answer is 50 miles per hour. But it is not. Let us assume that it is 120 miles to Birmingham (we choose 120 because it is easily divisible by 40 and 60). So it takes 2 hours to get there and 3 hours to get back. The combined journey of 240 miles takes exactly 5 hours. The average speed is therefore 240 divided by 5, which is 48 miles per hour. This is an example of where we cannot trust our instincts. A rigorous application of arithmetic is needed.

These problems show the power and precision we can gain by using elementary mathematical thinking. If we can state the problem in clear mathematical terms or if we can draw a diagram of the problem then it becomes much easier to grapple with. In the case of the average speeds it also shows that our first instincts can be misleading and the benefit of applying the rigour of mathematics. Here is another celebrated problem to illustrate this point:

The rope at the equator. The diameter of the Earth at the equator is about 8,000 miles (7,926 to be precise). Imagine a rope running exactly around the Earth at the equator. Now imagine a second rope that is exactly one foot higher than the first rope all the way around – you can think of it as being one foot off the ground or the sea. How much longer is the second rope than the first? Take a guess.

Most people think that the second rope would be much longer than the first – possibly many miles. If we apply a formula we learnt at school then we can find out the answer. The circumference of a circle is πd, where d is the diameter. So the first rope has a length of about 8,000π miles. The second rope has a diameter exactly 2 feet longer than the first. So its length is exactly 2π feet longer, ie about 6.3 feet longer (see Figure 14.1). The result is counter-intuitive, which just reinforces why we cannot always trust our natural judgements. We need to use some mathematics to be sure.

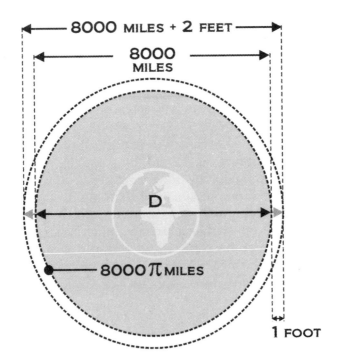

Figure 14.1   *Rope around the Earth*

If we can combine some lateral thinking with mathematics then we have a very potent problem-solving tool. Have a careful think about these two problems:

The tennis tournament. There are 123 players in a knockout tennis tournament. How many games will have to be played to complete the tournament and have one overall winner?

The bookshelf. There are six different books on a bookshelf. In how many different ways can the books be arranged on the shelf given that *Roget's Thesaurus* must always be to the left of the *Oxford Dictionary*?[2]

For each of these two problems there is a routine way to solve the problem and an elegant or lateral way. For the tennis tournament the routine method is first to calculate how close we are to a power of 2. If there were 128 players then we could play a first round of 64 games, then 32, then 16 and so on down to the final. By giving five players a bye and playing 59 games in the first round we get to play 32 games in round 2 and so on. So the answer is 59 + 32 + 16 + 8 + 4 + 2 + 1 = 122. But there is a smarter way of reaching this answer. Every match played has to produce one loser, and every player in the tournament except one, the champion, has to lose once. It follows that if there are N players there must be N−1 matches. So for 123 players there must be 122 matches.

Now let's consider the bookshelf problem. We can start with the thesaurus in the leftmost position and calculate how many permutations there are. Then we put it into the second position and calculate the number of permutations with the *Oxford Dictionary* to the right. We do this for the first five positions. When the thesaurus is in the sixth position it must be to the right of the dictionary, so the number of permutations here is 0. This method will secure us the answer. However, there is a more elegant approach. There are six books that can go in the first place. Once the first book is placed there are five books that can go in the second place and so on. So the total number of permutations is 6 × 5 × 4 × 3 × 2 × 1 = 720. In exactly half of these the thesaurus will be to the left of the dictionary and in half it will be to the right. So there are 360 ways of arranging the six books with the thesaurus to the left of the dictionary. The bookshelf problem is a perfect application of the principle of symmetry.

How can you refresh or improve your basic mathematical and numerical skills? Here are some ideas:

- Help your children with their homework – in mathematics and other subjects.
- Try the puzzles and brainteasers in newspapers and magazines.
- Try to calculate your bill at the shops when you buy a small number of items. Add the numbers in your head. Always figure out your change when you give a note and then check that you received the right change.
- Draw graphs and diagrams. Estimate the internal floor area of your house by drawing diagrams of the rooms and multiply out the areas.
- Estimate things. How many trips will it take you to mow the lawn? How many leaves do you think there are on a tree?
- Read some mathematics books. Choose the level that is right for you. You might even enjoy them!

NOTES

1. From Paul Sloane and Des MacHale (2003) *Sit and Solve Lateral Thinking Puzzles*, Sterling Publishing, New York.
2. Thanks to Des MacHale for this puzzle.

15

Get to grips with probability

Many people have little or no comprehension of elementary statistics or probability theory and their thinking suffers as a consequence. They make many errors that could be avoided by using basic statistics.

Try this real-life example, which has stumped many doctors. There is a deadly disease that affects 5 per cent of the population. There is a test for the disease and the test is pretty accurate. For someone who has the disease the test will give a positive result 90 per cent of the time and a negative result 10 per cent of the time. For someone who does not have the disease the test will give a negative result 90 per cent of the time and a positive result 10 per cent of the time. You take the test and the result comes back positive. What is the probability that you have the disease? Take a moment to think about this. It is a serious question and could mean the difference between life and death.

Most people and many doctors think it is highly likely that someone who tests positive will have the disease. They reason that if the test is accurate 90 per cent of the time for people who have the disease then if you test positive you have a 90 per cent chance of having the affliction. However, the real probability is much, much lower. Consider a random sample of 1,000 people who are tested for the disease. Since it affects 5 per cent of the population we know that 50 will have it and 950 will not. Of the 50 who have the disease 90 per cent, ie 45, will test positive and 5 will test negative (known as false negatives). Of the 950 who do not have the disease 90 per cent, ie 855, will test negative and 95 will test positive (false positives). So in total 140 of the 1,000 will test positive, but only 45 of those really have the disease. If you test positive the chances that you have the disease are 45 in 140, ie 32 per cent.[1] This kind of situation has occurred frequently. Many people, wrongly believing that they suffered from deadly sicknesses, undertook painful and damaging courses of treatment.

A good tool for handling this type of problem is a decision tree, as shown in Figure 15.1. The tree diagram shows all the possible outcomes, and you can attach numbers or percentages to each branch. This way you can add numbers, eg to see all the people who will get positive results. You can also calculate probabilities, eg by dividing the 45 who really have the disease by the 140 who tested positive to get the result of 32 per cent.

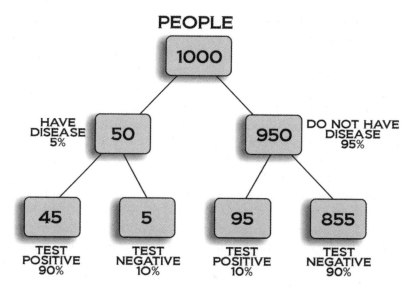

Figure 15.1 *Decision tree diagram*

At this point it is worth introducing three important concepts in probability. Events can be:

■ mutually exclusive;
■ independent – of each other;
■ conditional – one on another.

If you toss a coin it will come down either heads or tails. These two possibilities are mutually exclusive. If you draw a card from a pack it can be either a king or not a king. If events are mutually exclusive, when one event happens the other cannot. So the sum of their probabilities is 100 per cent.

'Independent' means just what it says. Now we can multiply the probabilities to calculate the likelihood of both events occurring. If the chance of it raining tomorrow is 1 in 3 and the chance of my winning the lottery is 1 in 10 million then the chance of both happening is 1 in 30 million.

Sometimes the outcome of a second event is conditional on the outcome of the first. If you draw two cards from a deck of cards, what is the likelihood that they will both be diamonds? The chance of the first being a diamond is 1 in 4. The chance of the second being a diamond given that the first is a diamond is 12 in 51. So the chance of them both being diamonds is 12 in 204.

A very useful concept to master is that of converse probability. For mutually exclusive events you subtract from 100 per cent the chance of one to get the other. If you throw a dice three times, what is the chance that at least one of the throws will be a six? There is a one in six chance that six will appear on any throw, so many people think that there are three in six chances of a six if you throw the dice three times. But on this basis if we threw the dice six times we would be certain to get a six, and we know this is not the case, so the reasoning has to be faulty. The proper approach is as follows:

Chance of throwing a six on one throw
$$= 1/6$$

Chance of not throwing a six on one throw
$$= 5/6$$

Chance of not throwing a six in three throws
$$= 5/6 \times 5/6 \times 5/6 = 125/216 = 0.58$$

Chance of throwing a six in three throws
$$= 1 - 0.58 = 42 \text{ per cent}$$

The principle is that you do not add probabilities of multiple independent events; you multiply the probabilities in order to find the likelihood that all the events will, or will not, take place. So if a horse is running in three races and the chances of it winning any one race are 1 in 3 then the chance of it winning all three races is 1 in 9. Many punters lose money because they overestimate the likelihood of a horse winning several races and they place accumulator bets.

Another famous example of how to apply the converse principle is the birthday problem. How many people should be present in a room before it is more likely than not that two of them share the same birthday?

Let's start with two people in the room. The probability that the two share the same birthday is 1 in 365 (ignoring leap years). So the converse is that the probability of the two people not sharing the same birthday is 364 in 365. When a third person enters the chance that his or her birthday is different, given that the first two are different, is 363 in 365. If a fourth person enters the chance that his or her birthday is different, given that the first three are different, is 362 in 365 and so on. So the compound probability for four people not sharing a birthday is:

$$364/365 \times 363/365 \times 362/365 = 98.4 \text{ per cent}$$

There is a 1.6 per cent chance that they share a birthday. We keep extending this calculation until the percentage chance drops below 50 per cent. The surprising result is that we need only 23 people in the room for this to be the case. With 23 or more people in the room it is more likely than not that two share a birthday.

Finally let us consider the gambler's fallacy, which is based on a faulty understanding of probability. It consists of the belief that deviations from the norm will even out over time and that this can help predict outcomes. So if the Mayfair square has not been landed on in the first half of a game of Monopoly, the fallacy would indicate that it is more likely than other squares to be landed on in the second half – thus 'evening things out'. Similarly, if red comes up five times in a row at roulette then the next roll is more likely to be black. This is reinforced by the fact that six reds in a row are highly unlikely. However, if the process is random then red and black are equally likely on the next roll.

A basic grasp of basic probability will serve you well in understanding risk, chances, statistics and gambling. It will help you to assess choices and opportunities in a more rational way. There are many books on the subject that will take you well past this brief excursion into the fascinating world of probability theory.

NOTE

1. For a more thorough examination of the treatment of conditional probabilities it is best to read about Bayes' theorem.

16

Think visually

Try these problems:

1. How can you arrange six matches so as to make four equilateral triangles of the same size?
2. How could you accurately estimate the width of a wide river if all you have is a single yardstick?
3. A fly is in one corner of a square room that measures 24 feet wide by 24 feet long by 8 feet high. A spider in the diametrically opposite corner of the room sees the fly and wants to take the shortest route across the walls, floor or ceiling to reach the fly. How long is the shortest route between the spider and the fly?

To solve these puzzles you need an element of visual or graphical thinking and in some cases some elementary geometry or trigonometry.

Can you think in terms of diagrams, charts, maps, graphs or drawings? Can you think in two dimensions, three dimensions or four dimensions? All right, so thinking in four dimensions is very tricky, but thinking in terms of pictures or diagrams is more than useful – it is essential for understanding and manipulating some issues. Verbal thinking or numerical thinking will not stand you in good stead for the problems above. We rely so heavily on the use of words to describe things that it is surprising how ineffective they can be for conveying information in some circumstances. Try describing an unusually shaped object such as an egg cup or a corkscrew or a coat hanger to someone without saying what the object is or is used for. Just describe it in terms of its shape. It is not easy to convey the information accurately. So when it comes to an unusually shaped object whose purpose is unknown we need pictures or diagrams.

In one of the exercises in my workshops one person has sight only of a picture of a house. He or she briefly describes the house and another person asks questions. The second person then has to draw the house based on the description and the answers to the questions he or she asked. It is difficult and frustrating but instructional. The exercise illustrates how poor people's questioning techniques are, how we make assumptions and how limited words are for conveying images.

Children are confident about drawing. They are happy to draw all sorts of things and nobody criticizes their drawings. As we grow older we become self-conscious about our drawings and lose confidence in drawing. We notice that a minority of people are skilled at art. They can draw well. Because other people are good at drawing we tend not to do it. But even if we draw poorly compared to artists we can still use diagrams to help us with thinking, problem solving and communicating. If a stranger stops you and asks for instructions to reach somewhere you will probably describe the route in terms of distances, left and right turns, landmarks and roads. If either of you has a map then you will point the route out on the map. So why not draw a little diagram? It would be much easier to understand. Try to give instructions using drawings – you might be surprised how effective it can be.

When taking notes in a lecture or meeting, try constructing a mind map. Tony Buzan popularized the concept of mind maps, and his book on the subject is recommended.[1] You start by drawing a simple image of the main topic in the centre of a sheet of paper. You then branch off for each of the main ideas associated with the topic, writing one word on the branch. Secondary ideas are added as branches off the main branches and so on. Many people find that drawing mind maps helps them to understand and remember material. Figure 16.1 shows a mind map about mind maps.

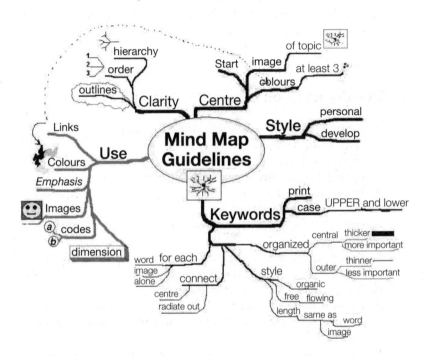

Figure 16.1   *Mind map example*

Another way to improve your graphical thinking is by taking a notebook with you and by making sketches. Try taking notes in drawings as well as with words. Your drawings can be childlike scrawls but that does not matter. By using your brain in this way you can express concepts that are hard to put into words. For example, say you wanted to change the layout of your office. A simple sketch is far more effective than a written explanation of the plan.

Many great artists, inventors and designers were visual thinkers. The inventor Nikola Tesla used images to help him design electric turbines to generate power. He would visualize a new turbine design in his imagination. He then operated it inside his head and used the power of his imagination to conceive how it would run and what faults might develop. He said it did not matter whether the turbine was tested in his head or in his workshop; the result would be the same.

Questionnaire on visual thinking

1. In the last month have you drawn a diagram to explain something to someone?
2. In the last week have you drawn a diagram to help yourself understand or remember something?
3. Have you visited two or more art galleries or museums in the last six months?
4. Do you like to study maps of places before you visit them?
5. Can you visualize what a landscape might be like by looking at the contour lines on the map?
6. Did you like geometry at school?
7. Do you enjoy manipulating your digital photographs? For example, do you crop and edit them to improve the images?
8. Can you use the 2D engineering drawings of an object or the 2D architectural plans for a building to visualize what the object or building might look like?
9. Have you worked on a jigsaw puzzle in the last year?
10. Do you use mind maps to record and remember things?

A score of 7 or more positive responses is good.

ANSWERS TO THE QUESTIONS

1. This is very difficult to solve in two dimensions but easy in three. Construct a pyramid (a tetrahedron to be precise) as shown in Figure 16.2.

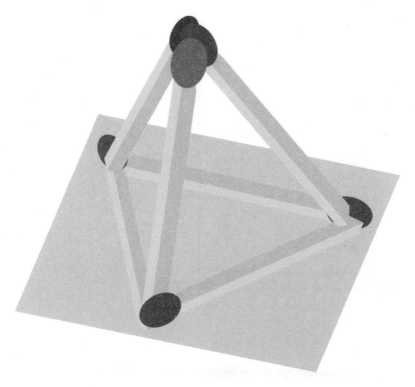

Figure 16.2   *Matches problem solution*

2. You can accurately estimate the width of the river from one bank using triangulation. Stand opposite some mark such as a tree on the opposite bank. If that is point A and you are at point B then you are trying to measure AB. Now pace along the bank perpendicularly to AB a measured distance (say 20 paces). Put the stick in the ground at this point and call it C. Now continue walking in the same direction the

same distance again (20 paces). This is point D. Now turn away at right angles and walk until you can line up the stick and the tree by line of sight. You are now at point E and the distance DE is equal to the distance AB because the two triangles ABC and CDE are identical, as shown in Figure 16.3.

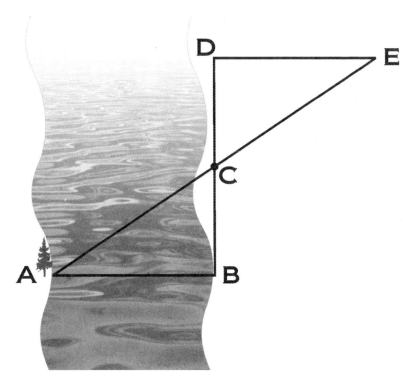

Figure 16.3   *River problem solution*

3. Once you draw out the diagram of the room as a plan view (Figure 16.4) then you can see that the spider has to go directly from A to F in the diagram. AB is 24 feet and BF is 8 + 24 = 32 feet. This means that ABF is a 3,4,5 right-angled triangle, so the distance AF is 40 feet.

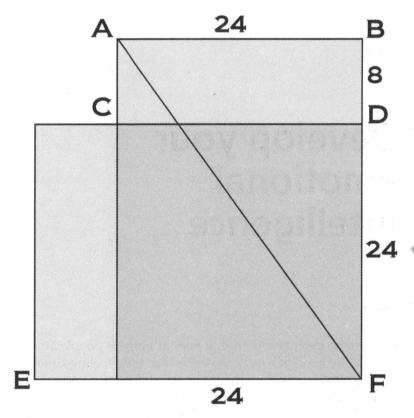

Figure 16.4   *Spider problem solution*

NOTE

1. Tony Buzan (2002) *How to Mind Map*, Thorsons, London.

17

Develop your emotional intelligence

It has often been observed that very intelligent people are not necessarily good at handling people and their feelings. Indeed it is one of the reasons why intelligence alone does not lead to success. The concept of emotional intelligence addresses this issue. Emotional intelligence is defined as the capacity to see, understand and manage the emotions of one's self, of others and of groups. Brilliant thinkers know that understanding and improving the connection between emotions and actions can help build their business and personal success.

Salovey and Mayer built on this definition by describing EI as 'the ability to perceive emotion, integrate emotion to facilitate thought, understand emotions, and to regulate emotions to promote personal growth'. Their model defined four types of skills:[1]

1. *Perceiving emotions* – the ability to detect and decipher emotions, including the ability to identify one's own emotions. Perceiving emotions represents a basic aspect of emotional

intelligence, as it makes all other processing of emotional information possible.

2. *Using emotions* – the ability to harness emotions to facilitate various cognitive activities, such as thinking and problem solving. The emotionally intelligent person can capitalize fully upon his or her changing moods in order to best fit the task at hand.

3. *Understanding emotions* – the ability to comprehend emotion language and to appreciate complicated relationships among emotions. For example, understanding emotions encompasses the ability to be sensitive to slight variations between emotions, and the ability to recognize and describe how emotions evolve over time.

4. *Managing emotions* – the ability to regulate emotions both in ourselves and in others. Therefore, the emotionally intelligent person can harness emotions, even negative ones, and manage them to achieve intended goals.

Daniel Goleman has developed a model of EI as a set of four key leadership skills:[2]

1. *self-awareness* – the ability to understand one's own emotions and recognize their impact;

2. *self-management* – the ability to control one's emotions and moods;

3. *social awareness* – the ability to see and understand other people's emotions;

4. *relationship management* – the ability to inspire, influence and develop others while managing conflict.

SELF-AWARENESS

There are many different emotions we can experience but they can all be put into one of five major categories. These are the major emotions – happiness, sadness, anger, shame and fear. So sadness would include depression, loneliness, hopelessness, dejection, dissatisfaction and so on. Shame would encompass guilt, remorse and feelings of worthlessness.

The first step in improving our emotional intelligence is becoming aware of our emotions and how they affect our behaviour and actions. We all feel emotions, but it takes some considered reflection to develop awareness of exactly what mood we were in and how it affected us. Sometimes the consequences of emotions are physical and clear to see – for example, you might blush when you feel embarrassed. Other emotions can produce behavioural consequences. When you feel angry you might become aggressive. When you are depressed you might become listless and demotivated. When you feel frightened you might be frozen into inaction. We need to understand how the moods that capture us alter our actions and responses. It is not that emotions are in themselves bad; we all have different emotions. The important thing is to analyse and understand what they do to us and how they change our attitudes and actions. People with highly developed emotional intelligence skills are able to recognize emotions in themselves and in others and to use this knowledge to their advantage.

SELF-MANAGEMENT

One useful approach is to write down some of the main moods that have affected us in the recent past and to link each mood to behaviours and responses that have resulted. You are looking to identify links. Many people find this an uncomfortable process, but the effort is worthwhile. You might observe that when you are criticized you become angry and then react aggressively. Now that you have seen the linkage you can ask yourself why this happens. More importantly, you can plan for it in the future. You can imagine a future meeting at which someone criticizes you – fairly or unfairly – and you can then run through various responses that you might adopt. Think through the possible scenarios including the one where you get angry and lash out. Choose the best scenario in terms of positive outcomes and rehearse it in your mind. When you are faced with this kind of situation take a short time out. Try to relax and take a deep breath and then rerun the approach that you rehearsed. It might involve channelling some of your anger towards energetic self-improvement. Great athletes practise their physical skills but they also rehearse situations in their heads time and time again. They try to feel all the emotions that they will experience when they get to that major final. By rehearsing they prepare themselves for success. We can do the same with situations that we can anticipate.

Self-talk is important here. We talk ourselves through the scenarios and coach ourselves into better behaviours and responses. 'The next time someone criticizes me, I am going to listen quietly and find something positive and constructive in what they say. I can learn from their comments. I will not attack them. I will thank them for their input.'

Some people find it useful to talk through their emotions and reactions with a confidant, maybe their partner or a coach, friend or mentor. If you can honestly describe exactly how you felt and how that affected your behaviour then the very action of talking about it can be cathartic. The two of you can discuss what happened and options for doing things better in the future.

SOCIAL AWARENESS

Social awareness is the ability to perceive, understand and react to the emotions that other people feel. Many people are so bound up in their own thoughts and feelings that they do not concentrate on closely observing other people. The key here is listening. We tend to multitask while we listen. We are doing other things, such as planning what we are going to say next. Real listening requires focused concentration on hearing what others say and observing how they say it. It means we must stop all the extraneous mental activities we normally indulge in when we are thinking about other things. When you

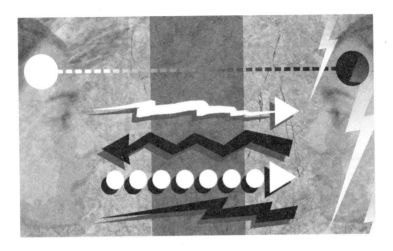

give someone your full attention you are paying that person a compliment and showing respect. He or she will probably notice and appreciate this.

You should observe the other person. Ask yourself the question 'How does this person feel right now?' We are capable of picking up very subtle, almost imperceptible signals that indicate how other people feel. Develop this skill. The best poker players have an amazing ability to read their opponents from the tiniest of indications. We need to develop a fraction of this skill. Carefully watch people's gestures, body language and tone of voice as well as listening to what they say. If in doubt you can always ask a simple question such as 'How do you feel about this?' or 'What was your reaction to this?' Do not play the psychiatrist and interrogate the other person but simply ask the occasional clarifying question.

Once you understand how the other person feels you can adjust your reaction depending on what you want to achieve. This can be done in a way that is constructive or manipulative. For example, if you are dealing with an employee who feels hurt and upset you can show empathy and sympathize with his or her issues before you move on to constructive suggestions. If you are debating with an opponent who gets angry when ridiculed then you can deliberately tweak his or her tail.

People do not operate on the basis of logic, reason and rational thought. They operate on emotions. Once you understand people's emotions you can manage your relationship with other people much better – to your mutual benefit.

RELATIONSHIP MANAGEMENT

You can use emotional intelligence in areas where different people interact. For example, it can help improve your relationship with your partner or improve the performance of your team at work.

As regards relationships with one other person such as your partner, a good place to start is by looking at arguments. Most couples argue – it is not necessarily a bad sign. You need to think about why you argue and what emotions underpin the arguments. Emotional urges can be very destructive in arguments. You should try to analyse why each of you feels the way that you do and what the results of those feelings are. If you can openly discuss your feelings – separately from the issues – then you can start to repair the situation.

Similarly in teams, there are group as well as individual emotions. We have all seen sports teams that are elated, motivated, angry, bewildered, deflated or depressed. Sports teams often show their emotions clearly. The team in the office can harbour a similar or wider range of emotions but not express them overtly. A good leader will read the signals, ask some quiet questions and understand how the team feels. He or she will then respond in a way that reflects the emotional issues the team faces as well as the business issues.

NOTES

1. Peter Salovey, Marc Brackett and John Mayer (2004) *Emotional Intelligence: Key readings on the Mayer and Salovey model*, National Professional Resources, Port Chester, NY.
2. Daniel Goleman (1999) *Emotional Intelligence*, Bloomsbury, London.

18

Be a brilliant conversationalist

You probably shy away from some people on social occasions. Their conversations are tedious. You groan inwardly when they approach for you know that they are unremittingly dull company. Equally you may be fortunate enough to know some brilliant conversationalists who can enliven any discussion and who are excellent company whatever the circumstances. In what category would other people place you? How can you improve your conversational skills to become a welcome sight at every party and social event you attend? How can you be a brilliant conversationalist as well as a brilliant thinker? Here are some pointers that might help.

ASK QUESTIONS

Most people prefer to talk about themselves rather than hear about you, so asking questions is a great way to start and to refresh conversations. If you meet someone for the first time, start by asking simple, non-threatening questions about them, what they do, where they live and so on. If you know someone moderately well then you should be aware of some of their interests, so simple questions about those are good ways to start. As you get to know people better you can ask more searching and interesting questions, for example 'What is the biggest challenge you have ever faced in your life?' or 'What is your greatest ambition?'

In a group, similar considerations apply. You should generally start new conversations by throwing out questions rather than making statements or talking about things you have done. By asking questions you draw other people in and engage them. It is said that small minds talk about people, moderate minds talk about events and great minds talk about ideas. By all means start the conversation with some small talk but once it is going be prepared to introduce some questions relating to issues and ideas. We will discuss where to get the ideas shortly. Obviously you have to judge the nature of the group first, so it is important to follow the next rule.

LISTEN

Great conversationalists are great listeners. Whether you are with one person or a group listen attentively. People like good listeners – wouldn't you rather speak with someone who was interested in what you had to say rather than someone who looked bored and indifferent? Also, when you listen you learn. When you are speaking you are not learning anything new. Make a conscious effort to focus on what people say. Show that you are interested by asking questions that support and develop the conversation: 'What do you mean exactly?' 'What happened next?' 'How did you feel about that?'

As you listen in a group, observe how people are reacting to the conversation. Are they engaged or ready for a change of topic? Is it time to move up from small talk to something more serious or time to lighten the mood with some humour? By listening and observing you can time your contribution to bolster the current conversation or move it forward to something new and interesting.

GIVE COMPLIMENTS

Pay compliments whenever you sincerely can. If someone looks smart or has lost weight or has a stylish new haircut then show that you have noticed by giving a genuine compliment. 'That colour really suits you.' 'You are looking very trim today.' If people tell you about some achievement, say at work or by one of their children, then congratulate them. As a matter of general courtesy and good manners you should always thank and compliment your hosts. Tell them what a great success the event is and how much you are enjoying it. Pick on some detail that they have chosen for the occasion that you like and tell them how well it has worked or how much you like it.

USE NAMES

Dale Carnegie, in his classic book *How to Win Friends and Influence People*, points out that people like to hear their own names. When you meet someone for the first time and learn that person's name, try to use it. 'So, John, where do you live?' Using the name helps you to remember it. It also shows that you are interested in the person. The same applies in larger groups. 'That is a good point you make, Mary, but have you considered...?' Mentioning the person by name is a subtle compliment.

KEEP UP TO DATE ON TOPICAL ISSUES

It is important to keep abreast of key current issues and topics in the news, entertainment, sports and politics. You should be ready to comment with questions, ideas, facts and opinions on the issues that other people are interested in. So see a few of the latest movies, read some of the most popular fiction and non-fiction, read the newspapers, watch the news, keep up with some major sports stories and watch some TV – but not too much. You do not need to slavishly follow every soap, but if someone asks you what your favourite TV programmes are then you should be able to list some popular and serious programmes and justify what it is you like about them. When discussing serious topics be prepared to oppose the conventional view and to take a rather provocative stance – even for the sake of doing so. This will lead to a more interesting conversation than if you just agree with what is said. For example, if everyone is against some political leader, then come to that person's defence with examples of strengths or achievements. If you want to introduce a contentious comment you can distance yourself from it by asking 'How would you answer someone who argued that...?' Make your points with conviction, evidence and, if possible, humour. But in a social environment be careful not to become belligerent or cantankerous. In general it is best to avoid really sensitive or controversial topics, especially if they risk offending people's personal feelings.

BE HUMOROUS

There is a place for serious discussion and there is a place for the light-hearted, so be ready to contribute in either environment. Witty comments tend to be spontaneous, clever and unexpected, so being witty is not an easy skill to develop, but there are some things you can do. Observe witty people in action and see how they contribute. Be bold enough to add your comments and witticisms and carefully watch reactions to see whether you are hitting the right note. Have a stock of funny stories. Do not force them into the conversation but have them ready when you get the cue or when there is a lull. Personal anecdotes relating to unusual experiences and misfortunes that befell you often go down well. Develop and practise some self-deprecating stories. Jokes, quotes and other people's witty remarks can also be used sparingly and with acknowledgement. But beware of smutty or offensive stories in mixed company. Laugh at other people's funny stories, even if you have heard them before, but never give away someone else's punchline.

SPEAK CLEARLY

Say what you have to say with clarity and enthusiasm. Many people mumble their words, or rush through them, or whisper so quietly that you have to strain to hear them. Good conversationalists are clear, articulate and easy to understand. They use interesting metaphors and visual images. Keep your sentences short and to the point. Don't hog the floor. When you have made your point pass the conversation on by letting others speak. If there is a pause then draw someone in with a question.

ENJOY IT

Be yourself, be natural and don't try to be anything that you are not. Approach the situation with a positive attitude and tell yourself that you are going to have a good time and meet some interesting people. Relax, smile and enjoy the occasion. People prefer to mix with the happy and good-natured rather than the grumpy and miserable. By all means have a couple of drinks but not too many or you risk undoing all your good work!

19

Win arguments

DOS, DON'TS AND SNEAKY TACTICS

There is not much point having brilliant ideas if we cannot persuade people of their value. Persuasive debaters can win arguments using the force of their reason and by the skilful deployment of many clever techniques. Here are some general dos and don'ts to help you win arguments, together with some sneaky tactics to be aware of.

Do

▪ *Stay calm.* Even if you get passionate about your point you must stay cool and in command of your emotions. If you lose your temper, you lose. When your opponent makes an inflammatory statement designed to provoke you do not react emotionally. Remain composed, smile and use questions or facts to rebut your opponent's case.

▪ *Use facts as evidence for your position.* Facts are hard to refute, so gather some pertinent data before the argument starts. Surveys, statistics, quotes from relevant people and results are useful arguments to deploy in support of your case. Careful research and preparation pay off if you can quote facts that put your opponent on the back foot.

■ *Ask questions.* If you can ask the right questions you can stay in control of the discussion and make your adversary scramble for answers. You can ask questions that challenge his or her point: 'What evidence do you have for that claim?' You can ask hypothetical questions that extrapolate a trend and give your opponent a difficulty: 'What would happen if every nation did that?' Another useful type of question is one that calmly provokes your foe: 'What is it about this that makes you so angry?' Try answering his or her questions with questions of your own. For example, if the other person asks 'Why do people spend so much time watching television when there are better things to do?', you could decline a direct answer and ask a preliminary question instead: 'What programmes do you watch on TV?' As the person responds to your questions it gives you time to construct your arguments and use some of his or her answers as part of your argument.

■ *Use logic.* Show how one idea follows another. Demonstrate that your reasons lead to your conclusions. Build your case logically. By the same token look for inconsistencies in your opponent's arguments and use logic to undermine his or her position. If for example your opponent argues that people are overweight because they watch too much television point out that he or she has not proved a link. Challenge assumptions. When people argue cause and effect then for each reason you can ask whether it is relevant, adequate, necessary or sufficient to support the conclusion they draw.

■ *Appeal to higher values.* As well as logic you can use a little emotion by appealing to worthy motives that are hard to disagree with: 'Shouldn't we all be working to make the world better and safer for our children?' Sometimes you can portray your adversary's motives as being more mundane, venal or selfish whereas yours are commendable and of high moral value.

■ *Listen carefully.* Many people are so focused on what they are going to say that they ignore their opponents and assume their opponents' arguments. It is essential to listen carefully. You will observe weaknesses and flaws in the position of opponents and sometimes you will hear something new and informative! If you listen thoroughly to the words opponents use and their sentences then you have the opportunity to repeat their words exactly, but with different emphasis. This can be a very effective challenge.

■ *Use relevant analogies.* People understand them and they can be powerful. Show how your analogy is linked and then draw out the lessons you want to show. 'Getting our office team to work effectively is like getting a kids' soccer team to perform. Both need communication, support and training. So we should have a coach and regular training sessions.' When your opponent uses an analogy look for the differences between the analogy and the issue at hand and be prepared to point them out or to offer a more relevant analogy.

■ *Be prepared to concede a good point.* Don't argue every point for the sake of it. If your adversary makes a valid point then agree but outweigh it with a different argument. This makes you look reasonable. 'I agree with you that prison does not reform prisoners. That is generally true, but prison still acts effectively as a deterrent and a punishment.'

■ *Study your opponent.* Know opponents' strengths, weaknesses, beliefs and values. You can appeal to their higher values. You can exploit their weaknesses by turning their arguments back on them.

■ *Look for a win win.* Be open-minded to a compromise position that accommodates your main points and some of your opponent's. You cannot both win in a boxing match but you can both win in a negotiation.

Don't

■ *Get personal.* Direct attacks on your opponent's lifestyle, integrity or honesty should be avoided. Attack the issue, not the person. If the other party attacks you then you can take the high ground, for example 'I am surprised at you making personal attacks like that. I think it would be better if we stuck to the main issue here rather than maligning people.'

■ *Get distracted.* Your opponent may try to throw you off the scent by introducing new and extraneous themes. You must be firm. 'That is an entirely different issue, which I am happy to discuss later. For the moment let's deal with the major issue at hand.'

■ *Water down your strong arguments with weak ones.* If you have three strong points and two weaker ones then it is probably best just to focus on the strong. Make your point convincingly and ask for agreement. If you carry on and use the weaker arguments then your opponent can rebut them and make your overall case look weaker.

Low, sneaky ways that some people use to win arguments

■ *Use punchy one-liners.* You can sometimes throw your opponent off his or her stride by interjecting a confident, concise cliché. Here are some good ones:
  – 'That begs the question.'
  – 'That is beside the point.'
  – 'You're being defensive.'
  – 'Don't compare apples and oranges.'
  – 'What are your parameters?'

■ *Ridicule and humiliate your opponent.* You see this in politics and on TV, so it can be tempting, but it is a poor tactic in the office or with friends and can cost you in the long term. It can be very effective in front of an audience but will never win over opponents themselves.

■ *Deliberately provoke your adversary.* Find something that makes your adversary angry and keep wheedling away on this point until the person loses his or her temper and so the argument. If you know the pressure points that cause people to become emotional and extreme then you can deliberately manipulate them. Other people can do it to you if you do not remain calm and considered.

- *Distract.* Throw in diversions that deflect the other person from his or her main point. When someone makes a good point you can say, 'That is all very well but what about...?', and you introduce a diversion. Skilful arguers will not allow themselves to be diverted and will return to the main point.
- *Exaggerate your opponent's position.* Take it way beyond its intended level and then show how ridiculous and unreasonable the exaggerated position is. If your opponent does this then calmly point out that what he or she is saying is not your position.
- *Contradict confidently.* Vigorously denounce each of your opponent's arguments as fallacious but select just one or two that you can defeat to prove the point. Then assume that you have won. You can handle this by remaining calm, asking questions, using facts and logic and appealing to higher values. In other words apply the 'Do' list above and do not be deflected.

Remember that an argument between two people is very different from a debate in front of an audience. In the first you are trying to win over the other person, so look for ways of building consensus and do not be belligerent in making your points. In front of an audience you can use all sorts of theatrical and rhetorical devices to bolster your case and belittle your adversary. In these circumstances humour is a highly effective tool, so prepare some clever lines in advance.

Questionnaire

Assess your argumentative skills with this questionnaire. Score one point for each positive answer and then total your score out of 10.

1. I enjoy vigorous discussions and debates on serious issues.
2. I always listen carefully to what the other person says.
3. I never lose my temper with people.
4. If I know that a contentious subject will arise then I research the topic in advance.
5. I study my opponent and assess his or her personal strengths and weaknesses.
6. I can appeal to people's emotions and higher values.
7. I can use logic to carefully build a case.
8. I always remain calm and in control even in heated discussions.
9. I try to understand the other person's arguments and sometimes change my mind on a point.
10. I like to find agreement even more than I like to win.

A score of 7 or more is good.

20

Ponder

We live in a busy, busy world. We are bombarded with information from all sides. The pressure to make quick decisions is intense, but the brilliant thinker will often take time to ponder quietly. Sometimes we need to slow down in order to speed up. A common problem with amateur golfers is that they swing too quickly. They snatch at the ball. Their coach will often advise them to slow down their swing in order to play a good, clean shot. The same advice applies to our thinking. Here are some ways to help you to slow down.

LISTEN

Many people are keen to offer solutions before they have heard the full problem. They jump to conclusions and race to their preferred answer. It is better to wait, listen carefully to all the data, analyse and understand the problem and then generate many ideas. When you are in conversation with someone who is describing a problem or issue keep asking questions and listening carefully to the answers before offering suggestions. Your questions will help both of you understand the problem in more depth and therefore will help you frame more and better solutions.

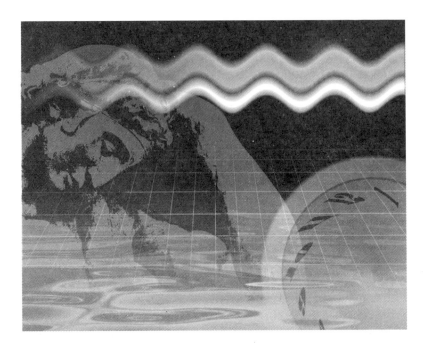

Don't take answers at face value. Ask for clarification. 'What did you mean by that?' 'Why is that?' 'How did that come about?' Keep up the gentle probing and, just like Agatha Christie's great mystery solver Miss Marple, you will get to the bottom of the problem. Each time we ask questions we are turning over more ground in our search for the treasure. We need to ask many questions before advancing hypotheses and solutions.

SLOW DOWN YOUR LIFE

Just because everyone else is rushing does not mean that you have to. Allocate some time each day for pondering. Take a long walk at lunchtime or in the evening and think about things. Clear away the clutter in your mind and think about some of the big issues in your life. Let your imagination conjure new ideas for tackling the big issues. Turn over the notions in your mind.

Even in a busy schedule we can allocate some time for contemplation. Think about key issues as you drive to work and use a dictaphone to capture your ideas. A five-minute pause at the beginning of the day is very useful to help us identify priorities and plan how we will approach things. Similarly, just before going to bed, it is very helpful to review some of the main items from the day, think about how we might have done things better and anticipate the key issues of tomorrow. Often deep insights and important ideas can be captured this way.

PRIORITIZE

Prioritize your tasks and focus on the most important. We tend to focus on the urgent rather than the important and so we put off working on the main things in favour of smaller things. We should try to eliminate the really small items, or delegate them, or do them quickly all together so that we have time for the important issues. See Chapter 27, 'Prioritize and focus'.

DECLUTTER

Remove the clutter from your desk, from your office, from your mind and from your life. Start with your desk. Remove all the papers and action them, file them or bin them. Be ruthlessly decisive. Take some time to go through your filing and delete anything that is no longer useful or needed. Now look at your diary. How many of the meetings and appointments that you have made in the last month were truly worthwhile? Can you eliminate some activities that offer little real value? Are there some clubs or committees that you attend out of a sense of duty rather than out of any real interest? Try to make space in your life and time in your day. If you can find a free half-hour each day for quiet contemplation then you can develop the power of pondering. You can reflect on the really important issues. You can prioritize.

DELAY SOME DECISIONS

We all know people who cannot make a decision – they can be infuriating. Decisiveness is one of the key qualities for great leaders. Someone who cannot make a decision cannot lead. So it may seem odd to advise that you delay decisions. General indecision and procrastination are not recommended here. But making very quick decisions is not always the best choice. Sometimes it makes sense to wait and ponder. Small decisions should be made quickly, but on bigger issues it is often better to admit 'I don't know just yet.' Gather some more input, speak to more people, think through the consequences or use a decision analysis tool. Taking some time can help you to reach a better decision and to avoid a catastrophic early misjudgement. For bigger items focus on making the best decision, not the quickest decision.

INCUBATE

Many great thinkers have testified to the power of incubation. The process looks like this:

- Understand the problem in as much detail as is appropriate.
- Register the need to find a solution but do not search for one immediately.
- Forget about the issue and do something else entirely, eg play a sport, go for a walk or visit a museum.
- Return to the challenge later and see what ideas now surface.

The power of the subconscious mind is amazing. It is like a powerful unseen computer that works while the main processor is recharging. So lodge a problem with the unseen computer and request an answer within 24 hours. You will be surprised at how often you receive delivery of a great idea.

MEDITATE

Meditation is a discipline that involves getting your mind to move outside regular thinking processes and into a deeper state of relaxation and consciousness. It sometimes means turning attention to a single point of reference. It has been practised for over 5,000 years and is an aspect of most major religions.

Meditation involves eliminating distractions and making the mind clear and composed. A good way to do this is with a simple breathing exercise. Sit in a comfortable position in a quiet place. The traditional posture is cross-legged but any other comfortable position is fine. Close your eyes and concentrate on your breathing. Count slowly to four as you breathe out and do the same as you breathe in. Exclude all other thoughts except the gentle rhythm of your breathing. As other thoughts intrude you push them away and think about slowly inhaling and exhaling. Eventually you will feel a sense of deep relaxation and inner peace. Stay in this state if you can. You should experience a calmness and feeling of space and tranquillity. The bustling problems of the world are set aside for a little while and you will feel unburdened.

ALLOCATE TIME FOR REFLECTION

Take your diary and plan some time for quiet, undisturbed thinking. We are so accustomed to frantic activity that it is difficult to go against normal culture and take quiet time for reflection. John Frost of Values Based Leadership recommends this method for reflection. You take time and ask four simple questions:

1. What happened and why did it happen in that way?
2. How did I think and feel about what happened?
3. What did I learn from this experience?
4. What will I change (behaviours, attitudes, etc) as a result of this learning?

Great thinkers allocate time for thinking. As we rush through life it is easy to keep making the same mistakes and to squander time on less important issues. By slowing down and deliberately pondering we can gain deeper insights and more profound thoughts. We can refocus on the most important priorities.

21

Maximize your memory

Read this list of words slowly and attentively. Alternatively have someone read it to you steadily and clearly. Concentrate on each word but do not try to commit the list to memory.

Plate	Mat	Table
Chair	Peg	Box
Shell	Cheese	Tomato
Spoon	Cord	Folder
Receipt	Binoculars	Anorak
Bottle	Tile	Kettle
Pepper	Shell	Radio
Astronomy	Sofa	Watch
Door	Cup	Picture
Shell	Map	Ambulance

There are 30 words in the list. Now close the book and write down as many of the words as you can remember.

Most people can remember around 10 to 15 words. If you wrote down more than this correctly then you did well. Which words did you remember? The chances are that the words you remembered fell into one of these categories:

- *Early or late on the list.* The first words fill our short-term memory from the front and some might stay there – 'plate', 'mat' and 'chair'. The last words are the most recent so some of them might stick – 'shell', 'map' and 'ambulance'.
- *Repeated.* The word 'shell' appears three times, and most people notice and remember that.
- *Difference.* Most of the words are routine household objects. The words 'binoculars', 'astronomy' and 'ambulance' all fall outside this category and are therefore more likely to be remembered.
- *Pairs that link.* If you noticed 'table' and 'chair' or 'cheese' and 'tomato' or 'radio' and 'astronomy' then these might have stuck in your memory.

By the same approach the words that you are least likely to remember are probably the mundane items in the middle of the list. Did you get any of these – 'cord', 'folder', 'tile', 'sofa' or 'cup'?

We can use some of these principles to improve our memory. Most obviously by repeatedly reading or saying something we improve our ability to recall it. This is a technique well known to students everywhere. We drill the important facts into our memories with constant repetition. The other methods are less familiar but equally effective. We can put our most important priorities first on our list. Our shopping list should be sorted so that the most vital items are at the top.

We can make things more memorable by making them outrageously different. So as you lie in bed at night you realize that the next morning you must post a letter, phone your mother and put the rubbish out. Exaggerate each image in your mind. Think of yourself struggling up the road carrying a huge letter to the letterbox. When you return the kitchen is full of rubbish from floor to ceiling. Just as you clear it you are deafened by the noise of a gigantic purple telephone ringing so loudly that the entire city can hear it. Your mother is calling you on the phone. If you now fall asleep with this sequence of images in your mind you are highly likely to remember it in the morning and with it the three important tasks.

Finally, linking pairs of ideas helps, as we shall see when we come to the memory pegging techniques. If we can associate a routine item with an outrageously different item then the memory of the outrageous item can help us to recall the routine item.

MEMORY PEGGING TECHNIQUES

Memory pegging techniques are particularly useful for re-membering numbered lists – and every list can be treated as a numbered list. We 'peg' each item to a visual symbol for its number.

One method is to use graphical representations of each number based on the shape of the number:

1. a pen;
2. a swan;
3. a pair of breasts;
4. a sailboat;
5. a fishing hook;
6. a golf club;
7. a cliff;
8. an hourglass;
9. a pipe for smoking;
10. a bat and ball.

Now let's try applying this method to the first 10 words in the list at the start of this chapter:

Plate
Mat
Table
Chair
Peg
Box
Shell

Cheese
Tomato
Spoon

We now construct extreme associations between the number images and the items. For instance:

- I am writing on an enormous white plate with a beautiful ink pen.
- A large white swan with a mat on its back swims into view. I can wipe my feet on the mat.
- I meet a very large woman who uses a table to support her breasts.
- I see a sailing boat with the captain sitting in a rocking chair on deck.
- As I pull up my fishing line I see a huge clothes peg on the hook.
- A large box is delivered and I open it to find a golf club – a 6 iron to be precise.
- I roll a giant shell off the edge of a cliff and it crashes into the rocks below.
- The hourglass does not run because it is filled with cheese.
- As I puff on my pipe little red tomatoes pop out instead of puffs of smoke.
- I am playing cricket holding a spoon instead of a bat.

Now we can easily recall the first 10 items in order. Furthermore we can clearly identify the number of any item. If we were asked what was the seventh item we simply think of the cliff and the giant shell immediately springs to mind.

An alternative to the graphical images of the numbers is a rhyming approach. Some people find it easier to remember numbers based on this type of aural linking:

1. Ton – one ton
2. Zoo
3. Tree

4. Door
5. Hive (with bees buzzing around)
6. Sticks
7. Heaven
8. Gate
9. Line
10. Den (eg the lion's den)
11. Soccer 11
12. Shelf
13. Hurting
14. Courting
15. Lifting
16. Licking
17. Leavening (baking bread)
18. Hating
19. Lightning
20. Plenty (horn of plenty)
21. 21-gun salute

So if we wanted to use this system to remember items 11 to 21 on the original list we might imagine:

- Cord – a boys' soccer team wrapped up tight with a length of cord.
- Folder – a shelf groaning under the weight of 1,000 yellow folders.
- Receipt – a sharp pain in my side caused by a very sharp rolled receipt for a knife.
- Binoculars – I am courting a beautiful girl but when I reach to kiss her a large pair of binoculars around my neck gets in the way.
- Anorak – I am in the Olympic weightlifting final wearing a large bright orange anorak.
- Bottle – I am licking a giant ice-lolly in the shape of a beer bottle.
- Tile – I am kneading the dough for a loaf of bread but find a roof tile in the mix.

- Kettle – I hate the kettle because I was scalded with boiling water.
- Pepper – I am sitting at the kitchen table when a bolt of lightning comes through the window and blasts the pepper pot into smithereens.
- Shell – a huge conical horn full of millions of shells.
- Radio – on the Queen's birthday she is greeted with a 21-gun salute but all the guns fire radio sets.

Choose whichever memory pegging method suits you better and practise it. The more ridiculous the mental images the more memorable they are.

What if you need to remember more than 21 items? There are a number of ways to handle this. One is with colours. The first 20 items are all black and white. The next 20 items are different shades of red. The next 20 are blues, and so on.

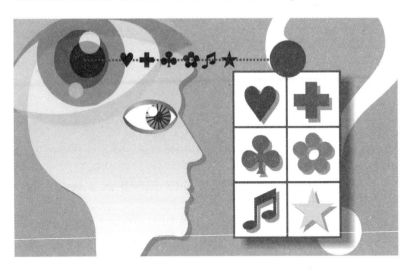

THE VIRTUAL JOURNEY

The virtual journey is a powerful and popular method for remembering lists of items. You take an imaginary journey around a familiar route – say your house and road – and you attach the things you want to remember to the places along the way. Say, for example, you want to remember a sequence of key points for a speech you are giving at your daughter's wedding. The first six items are:

- a story about her birth;
- a funny incident at school;
- what happened when the family went camping;
- her first date;
- how she met her future husband at university;
- a joke about husbands and housework.

The route you decide to take is as follows:

1. your bedroom;
2. your bathroom;
3. on the stairs;
4. in the kitchen;
5. on your front drive;
6. outside your neighbour's house.

So you might imagine a journey as follows. You wake up in your bedroom and hear a baby crying. You go into the bathroom and there is your daughter's headmistress sitting on the toilet. You cannot get to the top of the stairs because of a huge tent that covers the whole landing. When you go into the kitchen you see your daughter's first boyfriend washing the dishes. You then go outside and see your new son-in-law wearing a mortarboard and gown. As you pass your neighbour's house you see a line of men with vacuum cleaners cleaning the road. And so on for the whole speech.

When you come to make the speech you simply make the mental journey on the route and all the remarkable items will spring into mind in the right sequence. Each one reminds you of the story you want to tell. Many professional speakers use this technique. You can use it to remember a speech, give a presentation or recall a list. As before your should make the visual images dramatic and memorable – like the headmistress in the bathroom. With a little practice you will recall every detail flawlessly. People will be really impressed that you could remember every important point without any notes.

MNEMONICS

Mnemonics are simple devices to help the memory. They often take the form of a saying or rhyme whose words help indicate the information to be retrieved. For example, the mnemonic 'Richard of York gave battle in vain' gives the first letters of the colours of the visible spectrum – red, orange, yellow, green, blue, indigo, violet. Similarly you can remember the order of the planets starting nearest the Sun with the sentence 'Man, very early, made jars stand up nearly perpendicularly.' The planets are Mercury, Venus, Earth, Mars, Jupiter, Saturn, Uranus, Neptune and Pluto.

REMEMBERING NUMBERS

We can use a mnemonic technique to remember phone numbers or other numbers. Let each digit represent a letter: 1 = A, 2 = B, 3 = C, D = 4 and so on up to 9 = I. Suppose we have to remember the telephone number 0255 637892. We translate each number into its corresponding letter and we come up with O B E E F C G H I B. Now we construct a silly but vivid sentence using these letters. For example, Orange bananas eaten every Friday cure ghastly hangovers in Bolivia. This is much easier to remember than the number.

REMEMBERING NAMES

How often do you meet someone and then quickly forget his or her name? If you can remember someone's name then it increases your self-confidence, compliments the person and generally puts you on a better footing in the relationship. Here are some important tips to help you remember people's names:

- *Concentrate.* Listen hard when you hear someone's name and look at the person. Then immediately test yourself mentally to see if you heard the name.
- *Repeat the name soon after you hear it.* If Peter Jones introduces himself then ask a question like 'Where do you live, Peter?' The act of repeating the name helps to imprint it on your memory.
- *Comment on the name.* 'With a name like Jones I expect that you support Wales. Is that right, Peter?' This is easier to do with unusual names. If you are introduced to John Waladinga you might say, 'John Waladinga – that is an unusual name. Where does it come from?'
- *Make a rhyme with the name.* I met a thin man called Tony Cartwright and I mentally called him 'Bony Tony'. From then on it was easy to remember his name. Even if there is no connection you can invent an imaginary one for the rhyme: 'Pat with a funny hat', 'Roger the lodger' and so on. Of course do not speak these rhyming names in case they cause offence.
- *Make a picture story about the name.* For example, 'Bony Tony mends his cart to make it right.' Or if you meet Dennis Waterman you might think of him playing tennis on the surface of a lake. The more ridiculous the image in the story the easier it is to remember.
- *If you can't remember then ask again.* If you forget someone's name then the best thing is to say something like 'I know we were introduced but I cannot remember your name.' And this time remember it using one of the methods above.

Your memory is such a vital tool that it is essential that you develop and sharpen it. Practise memorizing things. Use mnemonics, virtual journeys, pegging and the other techniques here. You will quickly find that you can remember far more than before. And, for the important things that you cannot remember, make lists. The act of writing a list will help you to remember the things anyway.

22

Experiment, fail and learn

Brilliant thinkers learn in many different ways. They are receptive to new ideas from any source. They listen to the views of others with curiosity, openness and a degree of scepticism. They do not take things at face value. They will often view someone's new idea as a working hypothesis, something that might well be true but could be proved untrue. One thing that they trust more than most (but still not completely) is their own experience. They are more likely to believe something they have seen, heard, touched or felt than something they are told about second-hand. They value experience and seek it out as a source of new viewpoints, ideas and deeper understanding.

Scientists have always valued empirical knowledge, ie information gained by observation, experience or experiment, as opposed to theoretical information. Theories, predictions and calculated forecasts are based on assumptions, which can be wrong, so a central principle of the scientific method is that the most reliable evidence is that which is gathered through observation and experiment. Charles Darwin collected an enormous amount of empirical evidence during his long trip on the *Beagle*. He used it to build his theory of evolution.

The brilliant thinker values new experiences, experiments and first-hand observation to supplement and to check second- or third-hand sources of information. When we deliberately seek out new experiences we place ourselves outside our comfort zones. Whenever we try something new we take a chance. We run the risk of failure. When it comes to innovation, failure can be a stepping stone to success. Edison had countless failures in his experiments on the light bulb or the fuel cell, yet, as he said, 'Each one taught me a new way that did not work.' We can learn more from failure than from success.

What is the biggest mistake you have ever made in your whole life? Think carefully about it – even if the memories are painful. What lessons did you learn? Take a moment to write down what the error was and what you learnt. Great thinkers reflect deeply on things that went wrong as a guide to how to be better in the future. Now think about something important that happened yesterday or earlier in the week. It could have been a business meeting, a date, a discussion with your children, a speech or a presentation. To what extent did what you achieved fall short of the ideal? How could you have done things better? Write down your answers so as to articulate your thoughts clearly. If you spend some time on this exercise every week you will find many ways to improve your performance in the area you select.

Questionnaire on learning from mistakes

1. I deliberately seek out new experiences.
2. I like to try different places for my holidays.
3. I will often take a different route home just for the variety.

4. When things go wrong I analyse to see what I can learn.
5. I learn from my mistakes.
6. I try to ensure that I do not make the same mistake twice.
7. I take calculated risks.
8. I am comfortable in the knowledge that I will sometimes fail.
9. I do not mind making a fool of myself sometimes.
10. I do not find it difficult to apologize for my mistakes.

Give yourself one point for every question you agree with and rate your score out of 10. A score of 7 or more is good.

Trying new experiences means experimentation, exploration and taking chances. Many people find it uncomfortable. They would rather stick with what they know. If we stick with what we know then we are safer but we do not learn. Each new experience represents a learning opportunity. So here are some suggestions for new experiences to try:

1. At work be ready to volunteer for new responsibilities and tasks. Get a reputation as someone who is always game to try new things.
2. Visit the theatre or cinema and see something unexpected and different from your normal choice.
3. Go somewhere unusual on holiday. Try something well outside your normal scope.
4. Deliberately set out to meet new people and make new friends.
5. Turn off the TV and go to an evening class in something you know little about.
6. Learn a new skill, a musical instrument, a sport or a language.
7. Browse different internet sites from your favourites.
8. Read some magazines that you have never read before in entirely new fields.
9. Go to a lecture on a topic you know little about. (See what lectures you can attend at your nearest university.)
10. Visit a modern art gallery or an unusual museum.

Here are some examples of mistakes that people made and how they learnt from them:

- In the 1950s the Jacuzzi brothers developed a whirlpool bath, which they designed to treat people with arthritis. When it was launched it did not sell well. Very few people who suffered from arthritis could afford this costly item. They went back to the drawing board and relaunched the same product for a different target market – as a luxury social item for wealthy people. It became a big success.

■ Columbus tried something risky and new when he sailed west with the intention of finding a new route to India. He failed in his objective but found America instead.

■ Dom Perignon invented champagne when a bottle of wine accidentally had a secondary fermentation.

■ 3M invented a glue that did not stick. But Art Fry had the vision to see that it could be used as a marker, and the result was the Post-it note, a huge success for 3M.

■ During the 1920s and 1930s Alexander Fleming carried out research on bacteria. One of his laboratory dishes became contaminated with a mould. This was an unexpected result, so Fleming investigated it. The mould seemed to combat the bacteria. Fleming used the insights he gained from this accident to develop penicillin, which has saved countless lives.

■ Pfizer tested a new drug to relieve high blood pressure. Men in the test group reported that it was a failure as regards high blood pressure but it had one beneficial side effect. Viagra was a mistake that became one of the most successful pharmaceuticals of all time.

The examples in the box above are proof of the saying 'The wrong answer is the right answer to a different question.' Every time we fail we can learn something new. Failure is a much better teacher than success.

Think back to when you learnt to walk. You probably can't remember so let me tell you. You fell over many times but each time you got up and tried again. Eventually walking became second nature to you, but you learnt it originally by trying and failing many times. We need the same attitude throughout life.

23

Tell stories

We live in a world with information overload. We are flooded with data, facts, statistics and information in all forms. Definitive answers to specific questions are immediately available from search engines on the internet. But people want more than facts. They want understanding. They want meaning. They want context. They want stories. Children ask their parents to tell them stories because they like to fit the pieces of the story into a context they can understand. It is the same with adults. Audiences at conferences do not want to be bombarded with data and figures. They want stories with emotional impact that hold their interest and convey meaning. One of the most powerful ways to get your message across is by telling a story. One of the reasons that Christianity took hold is that Jesus conveyed his message not in sermons or theological discourses but in parables – he told stories that people could easily understand and repeat to others. Stories involve people, emotions, feelings, consequences and outcomes. They hold our interest because we want to find out what happens to the people in the stories.

When you want to communicate an important point then tell a tale. Compare these two approaches that a bank might use to let entrepreneurs know about business loans:

1. Last year we made over 15,000 loans to small businesses, with a total funding in excess of $1,200 million. On average we arranged the loans within 36 days of initial enquiry and we have streamlined our applications with online systems that speed processing. We have over 250 trained account managers to optimize customer service. In surveys of small business owners we are consistently rated one of the top five banks to deal with.

2. Last year we made over 15,000 loans to small businesses. One was to Gerry Martinez, who runs his own office fitting company. He is the 35-year-old son of Spanish immigrants and he had built his business to a level where he employs 20 people – including many of his relatives. He secured a major contract worth over $500,000 to refit the purchasing offices of a large retailer and he needed a loan of $50,000 to fund the stock and equipment required. Gerry was anxious because he was in danger of losing the contract if he could not secure the funding and he had been turned down by two other banks before coming to us. One of our most experienced advisers, Eddy Jordan, quickly assessed the situation and arranged the loan within seven working days of first meeting Gerry. Eddy was able to offer further help with insurances and in securing training grants for some of Gerry's apprentices. Gerry's business has doubled in turnover since he got the loan and he says, 'Thanks to your help, we pulled through a very difficult time and I am proud of what we have achieved.'

Which message is more likely to gain your interest? If you want a loan, which approach is more likely to convince you to look further into what the bank has to offer?

Anthropologists believe that storytelling has persisted in human culture because it promotes social cohesion among groups and serves as a valuable method to pass on knowledge to future generations. But some psychologists are starting to believe that stories have an important effect on individuals as well – the imaginary world may serve as a proving ground for vital social skills. 'If you're training to be a pilot, you spend time in a flight simulator,' says Keith Oatley, a professor of applied cognitive psychology at the University of Toronto. Preliminary research by Oatley and Mar suggests that stories may act as 'flight simulators' for social life. A 2006 study hinted at a connection between the enjoyment of stories and better social abilities. The researchers used both self-report and assessment tests to determine social ability and empathy among 94 students, whom they also surveyed for name recognition of authors who wrote narrative fiction and non-narrative non-fiction. They found that students who had had more exposure to fiction tended to perform better on social ability and empathy tests.[1]

How do you tell a story? Here are some simple steps to follow:

1. Introduce the characters. Stories involve people, so describe them.
2. Set the scene. This often involves some challenge or difficulty that has to be overcome.
3. Explain what happened next and how the situation resolved itself.
4. Draw out any conclusions or lessons learnt.

Go through your own life and think about some of your most vivid memories, some of the difficulties or problems you faced, and some of the funny or emotional things that happened to you. What were the lessons you learnt? We all have stories within us and sometimes we can enrich the lives of others if we tell a relevant story well. You have to be prepared to bare yourself, to share your feelings and frailties. But by doing this sincerely you can gain enormous respect and sympathy from your audience. Do not short-change your listeners; vividly describe your feelings, your emotions, your pain and your joy. They want to hear how bad it was, how scared you were, how surprised you were and what happiness you felt. Above all they want closure. They want to know what happened and why.

When in later life you think about your parents or grand-parents what you will most probably remember is not the facts about their lives or details of their earnings, wealth or qualifications. You will remember the stories they told you, esp-ecially heart-warming stories about when they were growing up, their relationships with their parents, the mistakes they made and the adventures they had.

Build your own store of interesting stories. Be prepared to tell them in social and business contexts. You can tell a personal story on all sorts of occasions – on a date or when giving a key-note talk. The stories that only you can tell are the best. But interesting stories about other people are also worth retelling if they are really amusing or make a great point. Keep a file or notebook with interesting stories and think creatively about how you can weave them into your work and conversation.

E M Forster explained it very simply. A fact is 'The queen died and the king died.' A story is 'The queen died and the king died of a broken heart.' When you want to convey a message, don't think just in terms of giving information. Ask yourself how you can illustrate the message with examples and tales. Use fewer facts and more stories.

NOTE

1. Jeremy Hsu (2008) The secrets of storytelling: why we love a good yarn, *Scientific American*, September.

24

Think humorously

As mentioned earlier, lateral thinking and humour are linked. Comedians take a different view of the world and ridicule the norms and standards that we take for granted. Jokes work by doing the unexpected or by going somewhere in the narrative that surprises us. Take this one-liner: 'I have a regular routine every night – hot chocolate at 10, in bed by 11, home by midnight.' The unexpected third leg of the story is what makes it funny.

Humour is helpful to us in seeing things in new ways, but it also has a battery of beneficial side effects. We can communicate a message much more powerfully if we include some humour alongside the serious stuff. If you can sprinkle your conversations and presentations with humour you will be more interesting and more popular. What's more, laughter itself is a powerful therapy. Laughter stimulates the release of endorphins, which relieve tension and make you feel better.

How can you get more humour into your life? Take time to read funny material; listen to comedy programmes on the radio; attend a comedy club. Associate with funny people who make you laugh. Make a note of funny things that happen to you and practise retelling them with relish. Sometimes the worse the calamity the funnier it is when retold. Look at life through the eyes of a child. Children laugh all day; they have fun; they see the funny side of things. If we can learn to see the world in a similar way we can laugh at things too. The Roman philosopher Seneca said, 'It better benefits a man to laugh at life than to lament over it.'

HOW TO TELL A JOKE

Many people shy away from telling jokes because they once told one that fell flat or they are afraid of appearing silly or of offending someone. Jokes are canned humorous stories that are subtly different from personal anecdotes. With personal anecdotes you have the authority to tell them because they happened to you. Jokes are independent and in a sense artificial so you take a little risk when you launch into one. However, when told well, a joke can cause great amusement and lift the mood of the gathering. A speaker who puts some relevant and well-told jokes into his or her speech will be appreciated by the audience, who are often bored with bland presentations and are crying out for a little entertainment.

Here are some tips on how to tell a good joke:

1. *Select.* Choose three or four jokes that really tickled you from the internet or a joke book. If you are giving a talk or presentation look for ones that have some relevance (however slight) so that you can work them into the pitch. Have one or two generic or topical ones that you can use on any occasion.
2. *Practise.* Practise them aloud – in front of a mirror if possible. Deliver them with style, confidence and panache. For each joke focus on the punchline and ensure that you can deliver it word perfect.
3. *Choose your moment.* If there is a convenient hook in the conversation for one of your jokes you can introduce it then. Otherwise wait for a pause. Sometimes the most amusing jokes occur when people least expect the teller to tell a joke. So, if appropriate, be serious as you introduce the story and then catch your audience out with the punchline.

4. *Deliver slowly and with confidence.* Many people ruin jokes by rushing them, mumbling incoherently or just getting the words wrong. Your practice should have overcome this but there is still a temptation to hurry. Slow down a little. Try to pause for effect before you deliver the punchline. That can add enormously to the impact.
5. *Match the joke to the audience.* A joke that is hilarious with the guys on the seventh tee might well be a disaster at the church bazaar. Jokes often challenge taboos, so it is OK to risk a tiny amount of offence to one or two people. But if your joke seriously offends people then you were guilty of misjudgement. In mixed company during the day you should stay with safe material. In the evening you can be a little more risqué, and with the men in the bar you can be outrageous. Choose wisely.
6. *Reciprocate.* Never finish anyone else's joke. Always laugh or smile even if you have heard it before. Be a good joke teller and receiver.
7. *Develop.* As you build experience and confidence try more and different jokes. But don't overdo it. Don't hog the conversation with one joke after another. A few really good jokes that you can tell with perfect confidence are the aim.

Finally, have some one-liners to throw in from time to time. Here are a couple to get you going: 'Velcro – what a rip-off!' and 'I enjoy long walks – especially when they are taken by people who annoy me.'

Funny jokes make the world a more interesting place. Enjoy your joke telling!

25

Think positively

In a study at the Mayo Clinic in Rochester, Minnesota, patients were given a personality test that assessed their levels of optimism and pessimism. The progress of the patients was measured over 30 years and it was found that the optimists lived longer than average for their age and gender while the pessimists had a shorter-than-average life. Researchers found that optimism strengthens the immune system and helps people to adopt healthier lifestyles. Optimists feel better about themselves and take better care of themselves. Pessimists confirm their fears by having higher blood pressure, more anxiety and depression.[1]

You can be a brilliant thinker with depressing, negative thoughts or a brilliant thinker with inspirational, positive thoughts. Your attitude determines your mindset, which determines your behaviours and the outcomes in your life. Many studies show that you will achieve more, feel happier and live longer if you choose the positive option. There is a wealth of books and articles on positive thinking. Here are some of the key precepts in those books:

1. *Believe in yourself.* These are the first words in the best-seller *The Power of Positive Thinking* by Norman Vincent Peale. Successful people start with a deep inner self-belief.

It has been shown that self-belief is more important than intelligence, education or connections in terms of lifelong achievement. The important starting point is your conviction that you are capable of significant achievement or that you have something special to contribute.

2. *Set clear goals.* This is explained in detail in Chapter 26, 'Set goals'. If you have no destination then your journey is haphazard. If you write down ambitious but achievable goals then you are already on the road to accomplishing them.

3. *Form a mental picture of your success.* Imagine yourself achieving your goals. Savour the experience of your book being published, of making the sale, of giving the speech to rapturous applause, of winning the race or of living your dream. As your mind comes to terms with this picture it will help you to put in place the steps to achieve it.

4. *Take ownership and responsibility for your life.* Don't be a victim. Don't blame others or circumstances. You are the captain of the boat and you decide where it goes and what happens. If you are not happy with an aspect of your life then form a plan to change it and take action.

5. *Talk to yourself.* Become your own motivator by telling yourself positive things. For example, at the start of the day you might say to yourself 'I am going to do really well today' or 'I am going to make real progress towards my goals.' When things go wrong or you falter then don't make excuses. Say something like this: 'That was my fault but I can learn from that setback.'

6. *Eliminate the negative.* Use positive self-talk to overcome the doubts and negative thoughts that creep into your mind. Deliberately eliminate worries about difficulties and obstacles by taking a positive attitude: 'I can overcome this challenge.' You do not ignore problems – you face up to them with a constructive and optimistic attitude.

7. *Associate with positive people.* Among your friends, relatives and associates there are probably some upbeat, positive, optimistic, dynamic people and some downbeat, negative,

pessimistic or cynical people. Think about them for a moment and select examples of each. Quite simply you should spend more time with the positive people and less time with the negative people. The optimists will inspire and encourage you. The pessimists will feed your doubts and make you depressed.

8. *Count your blessings.* Draw up an assets and liabilities sheet for yourself. If you are educated, in work, healthy, in a loving relationship, financially solvent and so on then put these on the assets list. If you are unemployed, ill, in a toxic relationship, bankrupt and so on then put these items into your liabilities list. The chances are that your assets will far outweigh your liabilities. We tend to take all the good things in our lives for granted and focus on our failings and needs. Every so often you should take stock and remind yourself how lucky you are to be alive right now with all the good things you have.

9. *Find the silver lining.* Learn to look for the opportunities in every situation that comes along. There are many self-employed consultants who will tell you that being made redundant was the best thing that ever happened to them. At the time it seemed a terrible blow but now they have found greater fulfilment and satisfaction in what they do. Every change brings good as well as bad, opportunities as well as threats. The people who do well in life are the ones who use setbacks as springboards for new success. Don't become depressed because you have not succeeded the first or second time. Take a break and then try again – this time a different way.

10. *Relax and enjoy life more.* Lighten up a little. If you can laugh at things then you can cope with them more easily. Don't try to do everything at once. Don't become overburdened with work. Deliberately give yourself little treats and do things that make you smile. Laughter is the best medicine – and the cheapest! Try to get a balance between work, exercise, relationships and play. Your goals will help here. The positive thinker looks for ways of gaining happiness and satisfaction in many small things – a walk in the woods, reading a story to a child, a glass of wine with a friend, a comedy on TV.

11. *Fake it.* If all else fails then fake it. If you are really worried, nervous or doubtful then pretend that you are confident and self-assured. Stride to the lectern, smile at the audience and act as though you are positive, professional and successful. Acting the role helps you develop the attitudes and behaviours that go with the part. You can fool the audience. More importantly, you can fool your brain – you will start to be the confident, positive person that you are acting.

If positive thinkers achieve more, live longer and are happier than negative thinkers then why would anyone choose to be a negative thinker? The answer is that many people find negative thinking to be an easy option that is more comfortable and offers less challenge. Do not fall into that trap. In your thinking, be brilliant and be positive.

NOTE

1. Maggie Greenwood-Robinson (2003) *20/20 Thinking*, p 96, Avery, New York.

26

Set goals

Do you write your goals on paper? Many people set themselves no goals at all. Others have a few unarticulated goals in their minds. All the evidence shows that people who write down their objectives are more likely to achieve them than those who do not write anything down. Successful people set themselves clear written goals and then break them down into manageable intermediate targets so that they can measure progress along the way. It appears that the act of writing produces a greater sense of commitment. Once the goals are written and then broken down into mileposts they become more real and more important to you.

In how many different areas of your life do you set goals? For those who write down their goals, many restrict themselves to just a couple of work-related goals and maybe a personal goal, eg to lose weight. It is recommended that you set goals in six different areas in your life:

1. *Career.* What do you want to achieve in your work? What are your ambitions for success in your work, for promotion, for recognition, etc? Write out your plans and think about discussing some of them with your boss.

2. *Relationships.* At every stage in life we should think about our relationships and how we can improve them. Think about your relationship with your parents, your brothers or sisters, your children, your friends, your neighbours and so on. Are there aspects that need to be repaired or developed? For many people the most important relationship will be with their partner. If you would like to find a partner then set this as a written goal. If you need to sort out an existing relationship, think about how it could be improved and plan the actions you can take to make it better. Don't just blame the other person for the problems. There is always something you can do to help.

3. *Health.* This might be the single most important area, since everything else depends on your continued good health. Most people know the key issues that affect their health (if you do not then your first objective is to get a health check), but often they do little about them. Set yourself clear goals to change your lifestyle in the areas that are deleterious to your well-being.

4. *Wealth.* Set clear goals for improving your financial security. This should include savings, loan reduction, pension planning, your property, your investments and so on.

5. *Personal development.* What are the skills and experiences you want to develop? Maybe you want to improve your public speaking, play the trumpet better, become a pastry chef or master sailing. It is important to keep learning new skills, and the best way to make this happen is to plan for it in your goals.

6. *Social life.* Many people find that they are so busy with work and domestic chores that they never have time to develop the social life, activities and relationships that they would like. If you want new friends, more visits to the theatre, interesting vacations and so on then you have to plan for it and set objectives. If you leave it to chance it may never happen.

How should you set your goals? Here is some general advice:

1. *Set yourself SMART goals.* Have targets that are specific, measurable, attainable, realistic and timely. Vague objectives are not helpful. You need to write down goals that are precise and detailed with dates and numbers.
2. *As a piece of counter-cultural thinking Dustin Wax advises that you should also set yourself some DUMB goals.*[1] These are aims that are dangerously unachievable and monstrously big. This may look facetious but there is an element of truth in the notion that we need some really ambitious goals as well as the attainable.
3. *Break down the goals.* Whether you start with huge targets or reasonable ones the next stage is to break them down into small steps so that you can plan and measure progress against each one. So if your aim is to lose 12 pounds in weight then one pound per month for the next 12 months is one way to break that down into manageable chunks. Similarly if you want to write a book set yourself the goal of say one chapter a week or 800 words per day.
4. *Don't get disheartened.* We all miss goals from time to time. The critical thing is not to give up. We simply reschedule. We take a look at what went wrong, think up some brilliant ideas to handle it and then set a revised target.

Use the Pareto principle to focus on your top goals; it says that 80 per cent of the value you generate comes from 20 per cent of your activities. Take some time to look at all the items on your goals or your to-do list. Sort them into order, with the most important first. What are the top three most important things you want to achieve? What are the things that will move you forward the most? These are the ones to focus on. How we can improve our focus and prioritization is the subject of the next chapter.

NOTE

1. Dustin Wax (2008) Get DUMB! The value of unattainable goals, Stepcase Lifehack website, 12 December, http://www.lifehack. org/articles/productivity/get-dumb-the-value-of-unattainable-goals.html.

27

Prioritize and focus

A brilliant thinker can apply his or her brain to many different issues and problems. The fact that the mind is open to a wide range of ideas and stimuli is a strength. But there is a paradox here. While being receptive to a variety of inputs, the brilliant thinker also knows the benefit of being able to focus on just a

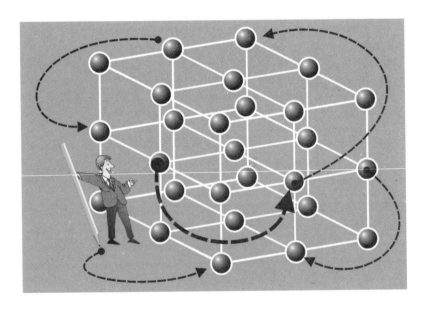

handful of the most important topics. He or she knows that the greatest payback comes from exercising the mind on the most significant issues and not letting minor tasks get in the way of the major priorities.

Just writing out a list of your tasks means that you can quickly prioritize them. There are thorough ways of prioritizing and one of the best known is the binary sort. Here you compare each pair of options in turn and give the more important one a point. After you have compared all possible pairings you add the points for each item. You then rank the items in order of their points.

For example, imagine that you have six unrelated tasks on your to-do list. In no particular order they are:

- Complete sales forecast.
- Read candidates' résumés.
- Answer customer's written complaint.
- Comment on new product specification.
- Review pricing proposal.
- Sign off expenses.

The first question to ask is whether any item is dependent on any other. They are not. The second is whether any can be delegated. Again they cannot. So now we compare each pair of options and give one point to the more important. Here we have written in the box our choice when we compare each pair of options:

	Résumés	Complaint	New product	Pricing	Expenses
Sales	Sales	Complaint	Sales	Pricing	Sales
Résumés	X	Complaint	New product	Pricing	Résumés
Complaint	X	X	Complaint	Complaint	Complaint
New product	X	X	X	Pricing	New product
Pricing	X	X	X	X	Pricing

The totals are as follows:

Customer complaint	5
Pricing proposal	4
Sales forecast	3
New product review	2
Candidates' résumés	1
Expenses	0

So that is the order of their prioritization. Some people would choose to do the shortest or easiest task first in order to get rid of the little items and 'clear the desk' for the major items later. However, this runs the risk of letting the most important things slide further away. If the most vital thing to do is to answer the customer complaint then it is best to do that first and ensure that it is out of the way.

HANDLING YOUR TO-DO LIST

There are many methods and books on how to prioritize, focus and manage your to-do list. Here is a summary of some of the best advice around:

1. *Apply the 80/20 rule – ruthlessly.* Doubtless you know the Pareto principle – that 80 per cent of your results come from 20 per cent of your efforts, or that 80 per cent of profits come from 20 per cent of customers. It is claimed to operate in nearly all walks of life, and empirical evidence would support it. For a teacher 20 per cent of the pupils take 80 per cent of his or her time. In a warehouse 80 per cent of the value is tied up in 20 per cent of the items, and so on. The corollary of the rule is that we spend 80 per cent of our time on things that produce only 20 per cent of our results. We have to ruthlessly reduce time spent on these things to free more time for the 20 per cent of activities that produce 80 per cent of our results. Start by listing what you spend your time on and then place a value against each of the main

things you do. If you can identify the 10 main uses of your time you will almost certainly find that only three or four are really critical and that at least five are of little value. How can you eliminate or delegate these items?

2. *Set goals.* See Chapter 26 on this.
3. *Continue to eliminate the low-value activities.* I know this is really the same as item 1 above but it is so important that it is worth revisiting. As we get under way with our goals the little things keep eating away at our time and preventing us from making substantial progress. Take an axe to the routine and irrelevant every week.
4. *Monitor and tackle procrastination.* Why is it that we put things off? Everyone does this. It is normal practice for us to put off difficult or unpleasant tasks. The important thing is to recognize this and take action. Target the main nasty task of the day – something important that we keep putting off. Some people call this the frog. The idea is that you eat it first because then anything else that happens that day cannot be as bad as eating a frog. Tackle it first thing and then give yourself a small reward. Another way to approach unpleasant jobs is to say to yourself that you will do it for just 10 minutes and then do something else. If you cannot face an hour of revision or exercise then just do 10 minutes. Often once you have started you will carry on for longer. See Chapter 28 for more on this topic.
5. *Delegate.* Give work to other people if this is possible. Outsource the activities that you are not good at. For example, you could have someone do your accounts, your filing, your photocopying and so on. You could pay an administrative assistant who works alongside you or you could use remote or virtual assistants. The internet offers enormous possibilities to use skilled freelancers. Ideally you should focus on those things that only you can do. Prioritize the areas where your skills and interests mean that you create the most value.
6. *Work on the most important things first.* Differentiate between the urgent and the important. A bill that has to be paid

today is urgent. Reducing your weight if you are obese is important. Every day, list the most important things to do and work on those first.

Bruce Lee said, 'The successful warrior is the average man, with laser-like focus.' If we set the right priorities and then focus relentlessly we can be victorious warriors in the battle against the enemies, distraction and procrastination.

28

Turn thinking into action

WHY PROCRASTINATION IS DANGEROUS

Most of this book has extolled the virtues of different kinds of thinking. It has counselled that careful analysis and sound thinking should be used before action is taken. Thinking is good. Just charging into action without a plan is generally a poor approach that will lead to poor results. But, just as all action and no thinking is bad, so too is all thinking and no action. There is a real trap that can catch serious thinkers. It involves the search for perfection leading to procrastination. Because we cannot conceive an ideal solution we keep searching and searching. We use one thinking tool after another as we analyse and assess the issue. We can easily fall into what is called paralysis by analysis. For most situations in life, there is a time for thought and a time for action. Even a professor of philosophy who is mulling over a grand new theory has to stop abstract thinking and start writing at some stage. When we over-analyse we can go round in circles and become stagnated in our thinking. It is then time to do something different and start moving, even if we are not sure of the best direction.

ASK YOURSELF 'WHY AM I STUCK?'

If you are stuck in a rut and cannot make a decision or take action then ask yourself why this has happened. Are you baffled by the problem? Are you scared of taking action? Are you lazy? Are you waiting for perfection? Are you worried about the costs or risks of taking action? Is there something in your mood or emotions that is holding you back? Be ruthlessly honest with yourself. Write down the reasons for your procrastination and you will see that most of them are feeble excuses. Focus on the serious issues and find ways to overcome them. Solve this problem the same way you solve other problems – with critical analysis and creative thinking.

IT IS ALL RIGHT NOT TO KNOW

Sometimes we have to admit to ourselves that it is all right not to know the answer. We cannot be right all the time and we cannot know everything. It is better to acknowledge that we do not have the solution right now and move forward on that basis than to wait eternally for the correct solution to appear.

DON'T WAIT FOR PERFECTION

The perfect can be the enemy of the good. If we keep searching for the perfect partner, the perfect house or the perfect job we can find that life has passed us by. We can strive for perfection but we must recognize that, although the journey is worthwhile, we will never arrive at the destination. It is the same with our thinking. We should be ambitious in our search for the best but if we insist on nothing less than perfection then we are heading for frustration. Constant improvement is a better goal than outright perfection. If we are moving in the right direction then we will get somewhere useful. There is a saying that is used to inspire writers, 'Don't get it right;

get it written.' It means that it is better to start writing and then correct and improve what you have done rather than to wait until you have completed all the research and planning you can possibly do. There is no limit to these preparations; you can always find something else relevant to study before you commit yourself. If you wait for the perfect time and the perfect conditions with every preparation in place then the chances are that you will never get started.

PHONE A FRIEND

Use a coach, mentor or friend as a sounding board. Discuss the issue with this person and openly share the problem that you have in moving forward. Choose someone who is discreet, honest and forthright. You need someone objective who can challenge your views and thinking. He or she will

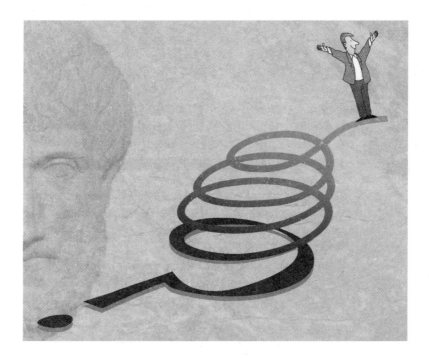

often suggest ideas or actions that can help. The discussion itself will help you to understand the challenge better and to understand yourself better. If you now agree to do certain things it is more likely that you will complete them because you do not want to admit to your friend the next time you see him or her that you have done nothing.

REMIND YOURSELF OF THE BENEFITS

Write down the benefits that will flow from completing the task. Perhaps it will help your finances, your prestige, your career, your relationships, your family, your social life, your health or your self-esteem. Each benefit is a reason for action. Follow this up with a list of the consequences if you fail to complete the task. Who suffers? How would you feel? Many people are more motivated by avoiding risks and negative consequences than by the rewards of achievement, so look at it both ways.

DO SOMETHING – GET INTO MOTION

There are times when it is very difficult if not impossible to make the right decision. Under these circumstances you have two major options. You can keep analysing, keep thinking, keep talking, look for more information and wait to see if things become clearer. Or you can deliberately take some action, see what happens and then revisit the decision. One question that can help you when faced with these two options is this: 'What is the worst that can happen if I take this action?' If there is a risk that you could lose your job, ruin your relationship or start a war then the action is almost certainly unwise. If the risk is manageable then you should consider action rather than inaction. Doing something produces momentum; it gives you a different view of the situation and injects some energy. The important thing is to watch what happens and be prepared to change direction if necessary. Do not be wedded to your first decision simply because you took it. If you can see that it is wrong then the sooner you correct it the better. Effective leaders are decisive but not stubborn. They know that changing your mind can be a sign of strength – not of weakness.

SET GOALS

A great way to overcome procrastination is to articulate your goals. Break them down into manageable targets and write them down. See Chapter 26 on this topic.

SHARE YOUR GOALS AND ACTIONS

Once we have told someone we are going to do something we are more likely to do it. The sense of commitment and obligation is higher. Share your goals and targets with someone supportive. Sometimes this person can be a partner in the activity. It is easier to go jogging in all weathers if you and your neighbour have a regular commitment to jog together. Share your goals and achievements. Celebrate every small success. It will keep you motivated.

PAUSE, DON'T STOP

The key message is that we should pause for breath, pause for analysis and pause for thought before taking action. We should think in terms of a pause, not a stop. This may seem like semantics, but the difference in mental approach is crucial. Whereas we can stop for an indefinitely long period, we pause with the deliberate intention of moving forward again soon. Brilliant thinkers spend time thinking and because of that they come up with more and better ideas. They select the best ideas and then put them into action.

MENTALLY REHEARSE AND THEN ACT

Many studies have found that people who mentally rehearse an action do significantly better than those who do not. The subconscious mind is powerful and it retains the positive images of the mental rehearsal. Before a presentation, a business meeting, a speech, a golf shot, a musical recital or an interview, practise the event in your mind. Imagine a perfect performance. Go through all the key aspects in your mind. Feel the sensation of success. This will bolster your self-confidence and dramatically increase the level of your real achievement. Mentally rehearse the action and then act.

Take the procrastination questionnaire

1. I often put things off until later.
2. I very rarely get through most of the items on my to-do list.
3. I sometimes feel frustrated at the end of the day because I could have done more.
4. I prefer doing enjoyable things to unpleasant but important things.
5. I know that I could have achieved a lot more in my life if I had put my mind to it.
6. I must have a detailed plan of action before starting any major project.
7. I focus on doing the important things first.
8. I write down my tasks and work through them systematically.
9. I like to get started on things even if I am not exactly sure how to do everything.
10. I enjoy accomplishing things.

Score one point for every negative (no) answer in the first six questions. Score one point for every positive (yes) answer in questions 7 to 10. What is your total score out of 10? Seven or more is good.

29

Common thinking errors

If your car develops a fault then you will probably notice it sooner or later. You may hear a rattle or feel a shake or the car may just grind to a halt. If your body develops weaknesses or illnesses then they will manifest themselves and you will probably take some form of remedy. Yet our thinking can be plagued by one of any number of well-known flaws and we can carry on oblivious to the poor decisions that result. It would be terrific if we could go for a thinking health check where someone checked our cognitive processes in the way that a doctor can check our bodily functions. Here are some of the thinking faults that afflict people.

THE AVAILABILITY ERROR

If you are driving and pass an accident on the road you will probably slow down and drive more safely for a while. A similar thing happens if you pass a police car. When people hear about a burglary they are more inclined to lock their doors and windows. When they hear about a lottery win they are more likely to buy a ticket.

When asked to rate the probability of different causes of death people tend to rate more 'newsworthy' events as more likely. People often rate the chance of death by plane crash higher after they have heard about a plane crash. The likelihood of natural disaster is overestimated because these events are more reported than more common causes of death.

We are heavily influenced by what we have heard or seen recently. We therefore place more value on the information that is immediately available. This leads to the availability error. In his book *Irrationality*, Stuart Sutherland gives the example of a psychology experiment in which people first had to learn a short list of words.[1] Some of the people learnt the words 'adventurous', 'self-confident', 'independent' and 'persistent'. A second group learnt the words 'reckless', 'conceited', 'aloof' and 'stubborn'. In a separate second task they were told to read a story. They all read the same story about a young man who had some dangerous hobbies, thought highly of his abilities, had few friends and rarely changed his mind once it was made up. They were then asked to describe the man. It was made very clear to all the people that learning the initial list of words had nothing to do with the second task concerning the story. However, those people who had learnt the first list of words gave a much more favourable description of the young man than those who had learnt the second list. The recently learnt words significantly affected how the people judged the man in an unconnected situation.

What we see first tends to influence us most. This was proved in an experiment in which some people were asked to quickly estimate the product of:

$$1 \times 2 \times 3 \times 4 \times 5 \times 6 \times 7 \times 8$$

A second group of people were asked to quickly estimate the product of:

$$8 \times 7 \times 6 \times 5 \times 4 \times 3 \times 2 \times 1$$

(Take a quick guess at what you think the answer is). The interesting result was that people in the first group consistently estimated a lower total than people in the second group. The average of the estimates of the first group was 512 and in the second group it was 2,250 – a big difference. People who see the small numbers first are influenced by those numbers to estimate a lower total than people who see large numbers first. The first numbers they see have a disproportionate impact. Incidentally both groups severely underestimated the correct answer, which is 40,320. What did you guess?

A common example of the availability error is when we use a memorable but unlikely piece of evidence rather than take a more balanced view. Someone might say, 'I don't think smoking is that bad because my Uncle Arthur smoked 20 cigarettes a day and he lived till he was 92.' The story of Uncle Arthur is available and memorable but highly unrepresentative of smokers as a whole. Similarly you hear people say things like 'Italians love gambling. I have known three Italians who were all heavy gamblers.' This person's opinion is heavily over-influenced by the three known Italians rather than the thousands of Italians who do not gamble.

MISTAKING THE CAUSE

In the 1930s an eminent medical journal published a report showing that cancer was much more frequent in New England, Minnesota and Wisconsin than it was in the Southern states. It was also more common in Switzerland and England than in Japan. It was known that people in New England, Minnesota and Wisconsin drank more milk than people in the Southern states. Also people in Switzerland and England drank much more milk than people in Japan. There was a strong statistical correlation between drinking milk and dying from cancer. The article concluded that drinking milk led to cancer. Many people saw the correlation as proof, but it was not. A deeper investigation showed that the milk-drinking regions were more prosperous and that people in general lived longer than in the regions where less milk was drunk. Cancer is a disease that mainly affects older people so it is not surprising that it has a higher incidence in places where people live longer.[2]

Similarly it has been shown that people who get university degrees earn significantly more over their lifetimes than people who do not have degrees. The conclusion that is drawn is that the degree directly leads to higher earnings. This conclusion has been used to justify loans rather than grants for students and even to proposals for special 'graduate taxes'. But is the conclusion justified? The people who get into universities have shown themselves to be intelligent, diligent, articulate and good at exams, at solving problems and at remembering things. These are all qualities that would help them to succeed in the modern workplace whether they had a degree or not.

It is not the degree itself that marks them out for success and higher earnings; it is the qualities they showed to get selected for the degree course.

Newspapers love to assign a cause to any effect. If incidences of leukaemia are higher in City A than in City B then there must be something wrong with City A that is causing the higher incidences. In the UK there was a suggestion of a possible link between a vaccination to prevent measles, mumps and rubella (the MMR injection) for babies and autism. Several newspapers published scare stories that exaggerated this claim, and although it was discredited by several thorough investigations the stories persisted. Many parents refused to let their babies have the MMR vaccination, with the result that a measles epidemic put many children's lives in danger.

We need constantly to guard against wrongly assigning causes. Consider what other possible causes might lead to the same outcome. Could a common factor lead to both cause and effect, eg to the degree and the higher earnings? Could an entirely different factor be the cause, eg cancer resulting from longer life expectancy and not from drinking milk?

THE GAMBLER'S FALLACY

The chance that three coins that are tossed all come down the same way is quite high – 1 in 4 in fact. The chance that 100 coins that are tossed all come down the same way is astronomically small. This is an instance of the law of large numbers. However, many people misinterpret this law to suppose that the cumulative odds sort themselves out in a rational and somehow deliberate way. This is the gambler's fallacy, as mentioned in Chapter 15, 'Get to grips with probability'. Just remember that coins, roulette wheels, dice and the like have no memory. They are not influenced by what went before.

THE CONFIRMATION BIAS

This is a tendency to seek information to confirm rather than challenge our theories. The work of Peter Wason, mentioned in Chapter 1, 'The need for different thinking', is a striking example of this. People will not look for evidence that disproves their theory – instead they gather evidence that supports it.

CLUSTERING ILLUSION

This is the tendency to see patterns where none actually exist. Because we like order and rationality we search for order and strive to find a cause for every effect. A study by Thomas Gilovich showed people were easily misled to think patterns existed in random sequences. The clustering illusion can result in superstitions, pseudoscience and conspiracy theories to explain entirely random events. The witch trials of the Middle Ages were examples of the desperate search for causes wrongly assigned to events. If there were a number of accidents in a community then a witch was found and blamed.

Cognitive biases

There are some 37 cognitive biases listed on Wikipedia. Here is a selection:

- *Bandwagon effect* – the tendency to do (or believe) things because many other people do (or believe) the same. Related to groupthink and herd behaviour.
- *Choice-supportive bias* – the tendency to remember one's choices as better than they actually were.
- *Conservatism bias* – the tendency to ignore the consequence of new evidence.
- *Endowment effect* – the fact that people often demand much more to give up an object than they would be willing to pay to acquire it.

- *Extreme aversion* – the tendency to avoid extremes, being more likely to choose an option if it is the intermediate choice.
- *Framing* – using a too narrow approach or description of the situation or issue. Also framing effect – drawing different conclusions based on how data are presented.
- *Hyperbolic discounting* – the tendency for people to have a stronger preference for more immediate pay-offs relative to later pay-offs, where the tendency increases the closer to the present both pay-offs are.
- *Illusion of control* – the tendency for human beings to believe they can control or at least influence outcomes that they clearly cannot.
- *Information bias* – the tendency to seek information even when it cannot affect action.
- *Need for closure* – the need to reach a verdict in important matters, to have an answer and to escape the feeling of doubt and uncertainty. The personal context (time or social pressure) might increase this bias.
- *Not invented here* – the tendency to ignore that a product or solution already exists, because its source is seen as an 'enemy' or as 'inferior'.
- *Outcome bias* – the tendency to judge a decision by its eventual outcome instead of based on the quality of the decision at the time it was made.
- *Post-purchase rationalization* – the tendency to persuade oneself through rational argument that a purchase was good value.
- *Reactance* – the urge to do the opposite of what someone wants you to do out of a need to resist a perceived attempt to constrain your freedom of choice.
- *Selective perception* – the tendency for expectations to affect perception.
- *Status quo bias* – the tendency for people to like things to stay relatively the same.
- *Wishful thinking* – the formation of beliefs and the making of decisions according to what is pleasing to imagine instead of by appeal to evidence or rationality.
- *Zero-risk bias* – preference for reducing a small risk to zero over a greater reduction in a larger risk.[3]

NOTES

1. Stuart Sutherland (2007) *Irrationality*, Pinter & Martin, London.
2. Sutherland, *Irrationality*, p 134.
3. Wikipedia.com, List of cognitive biases.

30

Boost your brain

The brain is an amazingly powerful and complex organ. There are about 100 billion neurons (nerve cells) in the brain and they can create over 100 trillion (10^{14}) synapses, which are the connections between cells. These synapses are the building blocks of our thoughts, ideas and memories. Your brain uses about a quarter of the calories you eat and a quarter of the oxygen you breathe. Think of it as the most powerful muscle in your body.

There is considerable evidence that exercising your mind helps to improve the functioning of the brain and fights mental decay. However, its exact effectiveness is not known. 'Playing games definitely works because you get better at playing them,' declares Earl Miller, Professor of Neuroscience at the Massachusetts Institute of Technology. 'The big question is do these skills generalize to normal everyday thoughts? That hasn't been studied.'[1] But many experts think that short-term memory, reaction time and general intelligence can be boosted by regular exercise, and it can also stem the onset of Alzheimer's and other debilitating mental illnesses. If we work the brain it appears that we can encourage the growth of new brain cells.

The brain reaches its peak capability in your late twenties, and then there is a long, slow decline in its functioning.

Physically it shrinks, and our thinking capability deteriorates. But with exercise we can slow that decline. 'There is growing awareness that challenging your brain can have positive effects,' says Dr Gene Cohen, Director of the Center on Aging, Health and Humanities at George Washington University. 'Every time you challenge your brain it will actually modify the brain. We can form new brain cells.'

The brain is highly adaptable and develops through repeated activity. So if you do crossword puzzles every day you will probably be almost as good at them at age 80 as you were at 30. Brain training games, puzzles, riddles, Sudoku, chess, Scrabble and so on are all excellent exercises. So is reading.

The author and neuroscientist Nancy Andreasen gives these four suggestions.[2] She advises that you should allocate 30 minutes a day to each:

1. Choose a new and unfamiliar area of knowledge and explore it in depth.
2. Spend some time meditating or just thinking.
3. Practise observing and describing things.
4. Practise imagining.

Ian Robertson, Professor of Psychology at Trinity College Dublin, says, 'The brain is plastic – it changes, and is physically sharpened according to the experience it has.'[3] He demonstrates this point with reference to the study of the brains of London taxi drivers carried out by Dr Eleanor McGuire in 2000. It found that their brains enlarged to help them store a detailed mental image of the city map. Brain scans showed that they had a larger hippocampus than normal. The hippocampus is associated with navigation. It grew larger the longer they spent working as taxi drivers.

Ian Robertson recommends reading out loud at breakfast, making lists of related objects (say blue ones, or those ending with A) and changing hands – brush your hair with your left hand if you're right-handed. These exercises make your brain work harder and cope with unfamiliar patterns.

How can you develop this muscle to something approaching its full potential? Here are some of the most important things to do:

1. *Use it or lose it.* If you lie in bed all the time you lose the strength in your muscles. If you watch TV all the time you lose the strength in your brain. Like any other muscle, the brain responds to healthy, vigorous exercise. Various studies have shown that people who actively use their brains are less likely to suffer from cognitive disorders, senility or Alzheimer's disease later in life. There are many different ways to challenge, stimulate and exercise your brain. Try some of the games mentioned in the next chapter.

2. *Feed your brain.* Research shows clearly that certain foods aid the functioning of the brain and others inhibit it. The best foods are fresh fruit and vegetables. They provide antioxidants, unrefined carbohydrates and folic acid. Whole grains, oatmeal and lentils help deliver thiamine and the right kinds of carbohydrates. Omega-3 fats found in oily fish and flaxseed oil are excellent food. You need proteins, which you can get from eggs, fish and lean meats. Vitamin D is essential too and this is provided by sunshine and some dairy products. At the same time you should drink plenty of water, fruit juice or herbal teas. On the other hand it is known that alcohol, most drugs, sugars and fats are bad for the brain – especially in high regular doses.[4]

3. *Keep learning.* The best way to exercise the brain is to keep learning – every day, every week, every year. You could take formal classes at night school or on training courses. You can study from books, CDs and DVDs or on the internet. Research shows that learning in itself helps develop the brain and prolong its use – regardless of the subject. It appears that better-educated people suffer less from mental disorders and degenerative brain diseases.

4. *Variety is the spice of life.* Doing the same thing over and over again does not give the brain the range of exercise that it needs. Variety in work, leisure activities, entertainment,

conversation, travel and social interests helps to stimulate and work the brain. Unusual activities employ the brain in new ways and make it learn to cope. For example, try turning this book upside down and reading it. It is a struggle for the brain to handle the new situation, but it does.

5. *Physical exercise.* Sports and physical exercise are good for the brain, not least by boosting the blood and oxygen supply to your head. A brisk walk or run is fine, but activities that require thought and coordination are better. Golfers who think about their swing and plan their shots or tennis players trying to outmanoeuvre their opponents are undertaking both physical and mental workouts. Similarly ballroom dancing, salsa, tango and line dancing are good because you have to concentrate on rhythms, steps, coordination and movement all at the same time.

6. *Sleep tight.* Sleep helps the brain and the body to refresh and recover. Sleeping on a problem can help you make better decisions. Sleep strengthens and improves our memory. Make sure that you get a good night's sleep. Take exercise, and avoid heavy foods or caffeine before bedtime. Sleep in a firm, comfortable bed in a well-ventilated, quiet room. A study in Canada found that students who studied for an exam and then had a full night's sleep remembered more and did better in the exam than students who stayed up all night studying.

7. *Read.* Reading good books, articles and magazines is one of the best ways to learn things and to stimulate your brain. Allocate time each day to serious reading. See Chapter 13, 'Develop your verbal thinking'.

8. *Remember.* Practise using your memory. Look at the exercises and methods in Chapter 21, 'Maximize your memory'. Work your memory every day and it will improve.

9. *Use numbers.* Deliberately do mental arithmetic every day. Use your calculator and computer less and your brain more. Check your bill at the supermarket or restaurant. Calculate your change whenever you give a note, and check it. Practise adding, subtracting, multiplying and dividing. It is a good workout for the brain.

10. *Listen to music.* Really listen. Music is a language that humans use to communicate. It is quite different from spoken language and it has almost universal appeal. Listening to music can develop and stimulate parts of the brain as well as change our mood. Whether you listen to classical, jazz, blues or pop, ask yourself 'What is the composer trying to say here and how is he or she saying it?' Separate out the different instruments, listen to their individual contributions and admire how the composer marries them to give the overall effect. Listen for melody, harmony, pitch, rhythm and timbre. Notice the use of repetition, development and contrast in musical themes. Can you detect the change from major to minor key? Can you spot chord sequences? The richness of music is amazing and we can all learn to appreciate music better.

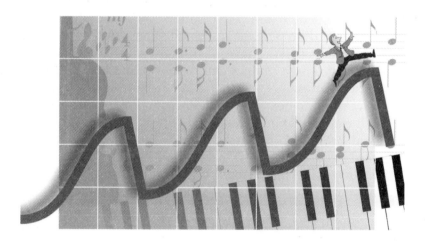

11. *Learn a foreign language.* The language we use helps shape the way the mind works. Learning another language and absorbing something of the culture of another country broadens the mind and helps us to see things in new ways. Revisit a language you learnt at school or take up a new one. Go to conversation classes. They are a terrific challenge, as your brain tries to cope with communication

under a different set of rules and with a limited word set. Watch some films in the foreign language. Read some newspapers, books or children's books. Get a pen pal in the country. Visit the country and try to speak to the locals in their language. The brain has to work twice as hard and yet it stretches and adapts to the challenge.

12. *Teach.* There is a saying, 'If you want to learn a subject then teach it.' For the thinker, teaching offers a great set of intellectual and personal challenges. How are you going to help the students to learn? Can you help them to discover or experience the lesson? How can you make it fascinating? If you do it right then they learn and you learn.

13. *Mix with intelligent people.* Spend time with people who are interesting, intellectual, well read, well informed, opinionated, stimulating and fun. If you do not know any then develop a plan to deliberately seek them out. Try to avoid people and conversations that are dull, routine and repetitive. Engage more with the people who raise interesting topics, have a different view of the world, challenge your opinions and make you think about things rather than people who talk about the humdrum and either have no opinions or agree with you all the time. It is not a question of being elitist or snobbish. It is about feeding your brain with the ideas and conversational challenges you need.

14. *Volunteer.* Do charity work to put yourself into a different situation where you can help people and at the same time learn from others.

15. *Sing.* Join a choir and learn to sing in harmony with other sections of the choir.

The message is clear. Your brain needs exercise, challenge and stimulation.

NOTES

1. Bryan Appleyard (2008) Can everyone be an Einstein?, *Sunday Times*, 16 November.
2. Appleyard, Can everyone be an Einstein?
3. Anna van Praagh (2008) Give your brain a workout, *Daily Telegraph*, 6 October.
4. *20/20 Thinking* by Maggie Greenwood-Robinson (Avery, New York, 2003) contains detailed lists of foods to be recommended or avoided.

31

Games for brilliant thinkers

Brilliant thinkers relish the challenge and stimulation of brilliant games. They enjoy games for the pure thrill of exercising their minds and judgements in pursuit of victory. You can take pleasure in any number of great games. As a child you probably played simple card games, draughts (or checkers) and noughts and crosses (or tic tac toe). Children develop many skills by playing games, but adults often lose this habit and therefore lose the opportunity for fun and brain exercise. Here is a selection of recommended pastimes. Add them to your Christmas list:

- *Chess.* Chess is the king of games. It represents a pure cerebral struggle between two minds. It teaches strategy, tactics, positional play and the benefits of absolute concentration. Every home should have a set. Every child should learn to play. Everyone can enjoy the challenge.
- *Scrabble.* Scrabble is the classic word game. You can play it with three, four or five people but it is ideal for couples. Luck plays a small part. You have to make the most of whatever letter tiles are in your hand using the available resources on the board. Skilled players see remarkable

possibilities and know a range of obscure and short words that they use adroitly.

■ *Monopoly.* This is the game that Fidel Castro banned when he came to power in Cuba because he saw it as a model for capitalism. There is a large element of luck but the skilled player will often triumph because he or she has focused on the right resources and developed a set quickly. It teaches trading skills and probabilities.

■ *Bridge.* There are many great card games but surely the finest is bridge. The bidding and the play of the cards represent two different skill sets, with the play having amazing subtleties. Good players remember all the cards played and can quickly deduce the lie of the hidden cards. Most players learn whist first before graduating to bridge.

■ *Cluedo.* This is a popular family game that is great fun. Can you put the clues together and figure out who is the murderer?

■ *Backgammon.* Backgammon is an excellent game for two players with its own mixture of luck, skill and gambling. You can choose risky or cagey strategies and double the value of the game on occasions.

■ *Poker.* Some people wrongly think that poker is all about bluffing. It is a highly demanding intellectual exercise in which the skilful players calculate probabilities and read their opponents. You need nerves of steel and excellent understanding of the statistics to succeed. This is a costly game to learn and it can be dangerous, but surely it is one of life's greatest pastimes.

■ *Dingbats.* Dingbats are rebuses or visual word puzzles where you have to figure out the common phrase or word represented by what you see. The advice is to say what you see – but can you look laterally enough to see the answer?

■ *Articulate.* This is an entertaining word game for friends and family to enjoy. You have to describe words quickly to your team members without any miming.

■ *Trivial Pursuit.* This is the daddy of all quiz games. This will test your general knowledge and your ability to think in the same clever ways that the puzzle-setters use.

- *Pictionary.* You have to draw the words in order to explain their meaning to your team mates. This will test your graphical thinking skills. It can be both frustrating and hilarious.
- *Charades.* Charades is a well-established game in which you have to mime the meanings of names, phrases or titles. You have to think quickly and find clever ways to get the message across without speaking.
- *Lateral thinking puzzles.* Lateral thinking puzzles are strange situations where one person knows the solution and others have to ask him or her questions. The quizmaster can answer only 'Yes', 'No' or 'Irrelevant'. You have to come at the problem from different directions, check your assumptions and put the clues together. It is good fun with friends and family.

If you want some excitement, challenge, competition and entertainment then take some time away from the television and get out an old-fashioned game to play with your friends and family.

32

Summary – a checklist for the brilliant thinker

Since the brilliant thinker uses questions more than answers here is a summary of key ideas from the book in the form of a list of 50 questions for you to ask yourself:

1. Am I prepared to consider the opposite of my most cherished beliefs?
2. Am I open to evidence that contradicts my assumptions?
3. How would a complete outsider view this situation?
4. Am I using the right tools to analyse problems?
5. How can I understand this issue better before attempting to solve it?
6. Am I continuously developing my verbal skills?
7. Am I confident with basic mathematical concepts?
8. Do I draw diagrams and pictures to help understand, communicate and explain?
9. Do I use mind maps to capture and express information?
10. Do I use newspapers and the internet to challenge my views or to confirm them?

11. Am I aware and in control of my emotions?
12. How can I approach this problem from a new direction?
13. What are the dominant assumptions here and what would happen if we reversed each of them?
14. Can I use a random word, object, visit, person or other input to help generate creative ideas?
15. Am I asking enough questions before leaping in with ideas?
16. What fresh and searching questions can I ask?
17. Do I listen carefully and attentively to the answers that people give?
18. What unusual combinations can I consider?
19. Can I use de Bono's six hats to look at this issue differently?
20. Am I using divergent thinking to generate ideas and convergent thinking to evaluate them?
21. Am I generating a large enough quantity of ideas before selecting?
22. Do I use criteria to help me select the best ideas?
23. Am I getting enough variety and stimulation in my experiences or am I doing the same things over and over?
24. How can I become better at conversations, networking, arguments and communicating ideas?

25. Am I reading enough good books?
26. Do I listen to a variety of music in a deliberate rather than casual fashion?
27. Do I pause to ponder major issues and let ideas incubate before making a decision?
28. Do I need to refresh my mathematical, statistical and probability skills?
29. Am I associating with positive people and taking a positive attitude to life?
30. Should I use a formal decision method such as ranked pair analysis?
31. Can I use mental hooks, virtual journeys and mnemonics to improve my memory?
32. Can I remember people's names better?
33. Am I visiting new places and meeting new people?
34. Do I deliberately learn from my mistakes?
35. Do I have a positive attitude towards risk and failure?
36. What stories can I use to teach and communicate?
37. How can I add more humour to my life?
38. Do I really believe that I can contribute something of value to the world?
39. Do I talk to myself as a stern, constructive coach would talk?
40. Am I thankful for all the good things in my life?
41. Do I have clear, written, SMART goals?
42. Am I focused on the most important things?
43. How can I overcome procrastination and get more things done?
44. Can I delegate or eliminate low-priority tasks?
45. Am I rigorous in my thinking or do I fall prey to thinking errors?
46. How can I have fun and give my brain more exercise?
47. Am I looking after my health and getting enough sleep?
48. Do I inspire, encourage and empower the people around me?
49. What are the key action items for me from this book?
50. If I could achieve anything in life what would it be?

If you keep asking questions, developing your skills, exercising your mind and approaching problems from new directions you can become a more effective thinker. Think differently; think better; be brilliant.

Appendix 1

Answers

WALLY TEST IN CHAPTER 3

1. Half-way – after that it is running out of the wood.
2. In total darkness none of the animals could see anything.
3. On the head.
4. The president would remain the president.
5. Neither – they both burn shorter.
6. The farmer had one large haystack.
7. BREAD.
8. He is still alive.
9. None. As soon as you eat one banana you no longer have an empty stomach.
10. A hole.

Only these answers count. How many did you get right? A score of 7 or more is very good.

MAN IN THE ELEVATOR PUZZLE IN CHAPTER 9

The man is a dwarf. He can reach the button in the elevator for the ground floor but can reach no higher than the button for the seventh floor.

Appendix 2

References and further reading

Adams, James (2001) *Conceptual Blockbusting*, Basic Books, New York

Bradberry, Travis and Greaves, Jean (2006) *The Emotional Intelligence Quick Book*, Simon & Schuster, New York

Buzan, Tony (1988) *Make the Most of Your Mind*, Pan, London

Buzan, Tony (2002) *How to Mind Map*, Thorsons, London

Carnegie, Dale (2007) *How to Win Friends and Influence People*, Vermilion, London

Claxton, Guy (1998) *Hare Brain, Tortoise Mind*, Fourth Estate, London

de Bono, Edward (1993) *Teach your Child to Think*, Penguin Books, London

de Bono, Edward (2000) *Six Thinking Hats*, 2nd edn, Penguin, London

Foster, Jack (2007) *How to Get Ideas*, Berrett-Koehler, San Francisco

Gelb, Michael (2000) *How to Think like Leonardo da Vinci*, Delta Trade, New York

Gladwell, Malcolm (2002) *The Tipping Point*, Abacus, London

Gladwell, Malcolm (2006) *Blink*, Penguin, London

Goleman, Daniel (1999) *Emotional Intelligence*, Bloomsbury, London

Greenwood-Robinson, Maggie (2003) *20/20 Thinking*, Avery, New York

Hsu, Jeremy (2008) The secrets of storytelling: why we love a good yarn, *Scientific American*, September

Jones, Morgan (1998) *The Thinker's Toolkit*, Three Rivers Press, New York

Levitt, Steven D and Dubner, Stephen J (2007) *Freakonomics*, Penguin, London

McCoy, Charles (2002) *Why Didn't I Think of That?*, Prentice Hall, Paramus, NJ

Peale, Norman Vincent (1990) *The Power of Positive Thinking*, Vermilion, London

Salovey, Peter, Brackett, Marc and Mayer, John (2004) *Emotional Intelligence: Key readings on the Mayer and Salovey model*, National Professional Resources, Port Chester, NY

Sloane, Paul (1991) *Lateral Thinking Puzzlers*, Sterling Publishing, New York

Sloane, Paul (2006) *The Leader's Guide to Lateral Thinking Skills*, Kogan Page, London

Sloane, Paul (2007) *The Innovative Leader*, Kogan Page, London

Sloane, Paul and MacHale, Des (1997) *Perplexing Lateral Thinking Puzzles*, Sterling Publishing, New York

Sloane, Paul and MacHale, Des (2003) *Sit and Solve Lateral Thinking Puzzles*, Sterling Publishing, New York

Sutherland, Stuart (2007) *Irrationality*, Pinter & Martin, London

Taleb, Nassim (2008) *The Black Swan*, Penguin, London

Wolff, Jurgen (2008) *Focus: The power of targeted thinking*, Prentice Hall, Harlow

Index

NB: page numbers in *italic* indicate figures or tables